CELEBRATION OF HAND-HOOKED RUGS XXIII

2013 Edition

Editor
Debra Smith

Author
Ayleen Stellhorn

Designer
CW Design Solutions, Inc.

Magazine Assistants
Candice R. Derr
Kathryn Fulton

Operations Manager
Anne Lodge

Publisher
Judith Schnell

Rug photographs provided by the artist unless otherwise noted.

Rug Hooking magazine is published five times a year in Jan./Feb., March/April/May, June/July/Aug., Sept./Oct., and Nov./Dec. by Stackpole, Inc., 5067 Ritter Road, Mechanicsburg, PA 17055. *Celebration of Hand-Hooked Rugs* is published annually. Contents Copyright© 2013. All rights reserved. Reproduction in whole or part without the written consent of the publisher is prohibited. Canadian GST #R137954772.

NOTICE: All patterns and hooked pieces presented here are Copyright© the individual designers, who are named in the corresponding captions. No hooked piece presented here may be duplicated in any form without the designer's consent.

A Publication of

R·U·G HOOKING

5067 Ritter Road
Mechanicsburg, PA 17055
(717) 796-0411
www.rughookingmagazine.com
rughook@stackpolebooks.com

ISBN-978-0-8117-1264-4

Printed in U.S.A.

9001081764

Welcome to Celebration XXIII

Once more *RHM* is pleased to bring you the annual *Celebration of Hand-Hooked Rugs*. This is the twenty-third volume of our series featuring some of the best hooked rugs created by rug hookers in the past two years.

Today's rug hookers are extraordinarily creative, as you will see when you page through this book. *Celebration XXIII* brings you a wide variety of rug styles—from traditional florals and crewels to riffs on modern day graffiti, from cozy primitive rugs to edgy contemporary designs. There is no limit to the creativity and skill of today's fiber artists.

In many ways, the *RHM* year revolves around the *Celebration* calendar. We put out the call for entries each September. By December the entries have arrived and as we prepare for the judging, which takes place in January, we admire the marvelous hooked pieces that are entered. In April, we are well into gathering all the photos and stories for the new *Celebration* book, and in August we publish and deliver that book to our readers and to the rest of the world. We mark the end of the *Celebration* year with our annual August trip to Sauder Village Rug Hooking Week and the *Celebration* exhibit in Foundry Hall.

That incredible show closes late Saturday afternoon and as we take the rugs down off the walls, we begin to focus on September, when it all begins again with a new call for entries. What new rugs will be entered? What fabulously inventive designs will we see? Which rugs will be our favorites—though, in truth, it is nearly impossible to pick a favorite because they all are masterpieces.

So turn the page and browse through this collection of wonderful hooked rugs. Let them inspire you and satisfy your love of all things wool and all things hooked. It is an honor for us to bring them to you in *Celebration XXIII*.

Debra Smith, Editor

D1605493

Readers' Choice
Remember to vote for your favorite hooked rugs to be a part of the Readers' Choice decision. You can vote either with the paper ballot included in this book, or digitally. Go to **www.rughookingmagazine.com,** and look for **Celebration Readers' Choice Voting**. Or use the enclosed ballot and return it to us by mail. We must have your vote by **December 31, 2013.**

On the Cover: Symphony, *hooked by Lynne Powell, 2012. For more information on this spectacular rug,* turn to page 80.

Table of Contents

20

120

58

RUGS BASED ON COMMERCIAL DESIGNS

104

134

RUGS BASED ON PRIMITIVE DESIGNS

HONORABLE MENTIONS

Meet the Judges

Each year a new panel of judges takes on the daunting task of evaluating *Celebration* entries. Imagine the enormity of the task: each entry comes with 4 separate photos, so in a field of 200 entries the judges will review and evaluate a total of 800 photographs. With our current system of online judging, the process is more judge-friendly than in the days when they traveled here to view the entries, one slide at a time. But consider the task that they face: even sitting in their own homes in a favorite chair with a cup of coffee nearby, it is an enormous commitment of time and energy. Hours and hours of concentration, deliberation, and careful consideration; the judges essentially commit one week in early January to *Celebration* judging. All for the love of rug hooking. It is their expertise and wide-ranging experience that makes *Celebration* work so well; they are the foundation of the whole enterprise.

And so we extend our heartfelt thanks to these four judges and to all the judges who have gone before them. And, please . . . if you have an opportunity, be sure to thank a judge. Their contributions cannot be overstated.

Jon Ciemiewicz

Jon started hooking rugs 18 years ago and, for the most part, is self taught. He hooked independently for the first four years, then began attending camps, workshops, and the McGown teachers' program. Jon has been traveling from his home in New Hampshire to teach workshops for the past 14 years throughout the United States and Canada. Several of his rugs have been chosen for inclusion in *Rug Hooking* magazine's *Celebration of Hand-Hooked Rugs* and have been selected as best in show at State Fairs.

April DeConick

April is an award-winning hooked wool artist and master dyer. Her hooked rugs and mats have appeared in *Rug Hooking* magazine's *Celebration of Hand-Hooked Rugs*, *Rug Hooking* magazine, and the *ATHA Newsletter*. Her rugs have received blue ribbon People's Choice Awards in 2011 and 2012 at the Sauder Village Rug Hooking Exhibition. She has authored articles for the *ATHA Newsletter* and *Rug Hooking* magazine and has written and fully illustrated the step-by-step instructional dye book *The Wool Palette: A Rug Hooker's Guide to Dyeing*

Your Own Color Palette of Wool. She blogs about her rug hooking adventures on Red Jack Rugs. April teaches classes in dyeing and hooked portraiture at retreats and camps and is the vice president of the Stash Sisters ATHA guild in Region 9. She began hooking in 1995 in rural Michigan and she currently resides in Houston, Texas, with her son, Alexander, and her husband, Wade.

Katie Hartner

Katie learned many fiber arts and crafts from her mother and grandmother as she was growing up with her two sisters. She discovered rug hooking in the late 1990s and has been "hooked" ever since. Since 2001, Katie has owned a brick and mortar quilt shop called A Nimble Thimble and sells Bernina sewing machines as well as rug hooking supplies. She began teaching rug hooking at A Nimble Thimble in 2003. She loves the creative expression rug hooking allows when approached with a free-form canvas, and she strives to foster individual interpretation in all of her students. Katie appreciates all aspects of rug hooking but primarily hooks primitives. Her work appeared in *Celebration XVIII*, and her work was selected as People's Choice, Primitive winner at Sauder Village Rug Hooking Week. She is on the Editorial Board of ATHA and is a codirector of Star of Texas Rug Camps.

Laura Pierce

Laura is a fourth generation rug hooker, growing up with rugs made by her mother, Emma Webber. Laura began hooking rugs in 1996 when a new ATHA chapter started up in Sonoma County. While primarily a wide-cut artist, Laura has completed rugs ranging in style from abstract to realistic, impressionistic to traditional. Her rugs have been featured in the *ATHA Newsletter*, *Rug Hooking* magazine, and Anne-Marie Littenberg's book, *Hooked Rug Portraits*. Her work also appears in art galleries. Laura teaches at her studio in Sonoma County, at rug camps around the country, and at workshops anywhere. Laura is past president of the ATHA chapter Wine Country Rug Hookers and is now serving as the ATHA Region 12 Representative. Laura earned her McGown Accreditation at Western Teachers' Workshop in 2006 and is currently director of Little River Inn Rug Camp and the Fiber Jam. Laura has written articles for *ATHA* and *Rug Hooking* magazine.

Alzheimer's Rug

Throughout her career as a rug hooking artist, Donna Hrkman has used her work to express certain feelings about causes that are important to her. This rug, *Alzheimer's Rug*, is her response to the devastation of that disease and pays tribute to her father-in-law, who struggled with and eventually succumbed to Alzheimer's.

Donna color planned the rug, focusing on dark, intense colors to indicate the sense of foreboding and turmoil facing the person who confronts the uncertainty of Alzheimer's. She chose dark, solid dyes, some spot dyes, and a few dip dyes to color the wool she needed. "In addition to the wool," she said, "I used bits of colored silk ribbon. The design illustrates the sense of 'coming apart' as a result of Alzheimer's, as the best and brightest parts of her are being pulled away. The bits of ribbon represent these bits of her personality."

As Donna designed this piece, she focused on the woman's face. "Her expression is a very important part of this rug," she said. "I wanted to capture that vacant look in her eyes that those of us with family members who suffer with Alzheimer's recognize."

Donna found getting the right background difficult and tried several different variations before she was satisfied. However, the most challenging part of this rug was not in the hooking. "The emotional nature of the theme was difficult to come to terms with," she said. "It brought back a lot of painful memories."

Donna plans to exhibit her rug at a clinic that specializes in treating Alzheimer's. "I think it's very important that women who create hooked rugs take the time at least once to create a rug that makes a statement or raises awareness about a cause they believe in," she said. "We, as artists, owe it to our community and our society to give back, using our rugs as our voice."

In the Judges' Words

- *Superb portraiture with strong message*
- *Powerful and emotional*
- *Great color and hooking*
- *Fantastic idea*

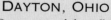

DONNA HRKMAN
DAYTON, OHIO

Donna resisted the pull of rug hooking for quite a while, but once she tried it she became completely engrossed. She estimates that she has most likely hooked over 100 rugs, mats, runners, and other pieces over the past 10 years. This is her sixth rug to be featured in Celebration.

Alzheimer's Rug, 29" x 23", #3- and 5-cut hand-dyed wool, ribbon, and yarn on linen.
Designed and hooked by Donna Hrkman, Dayton, Ohio, 2012.

BEElieve

Shawn Niemeyer recently started designing her own rug hooking projects, and she played with this design on paper for several months before she got it just right. Shawn started with a cluster of realistic flowers in the center of the rug and then boxed them in with a colorful, four-part inner border. In each section of the border she wrote a word: love, hope, joy, wish. The dark background behind the flowers continues to the outer border of the rug where flowing lines contrast with the straight lines of the inner border. "I couldn't wait to get started on it, once I was finally satisfied with the pattern," she said.

Shawn finds color planning to be paralyzing, but with this design, she had a clear idea of the colors she wanted to use. The bright colors of the flowers in the center had to be balanced with a very dark background, then a colorful

hit-and-miss border would include more bright colors to enhance the flowers. She chose a combination of recycled, off-the-bolt, and dyed wool to bring her idea to fruition.

Most of the wool was casserole dyed, but Shawn also experimented with microwave dyeing and loved the quickness and limited mess it leaves behind. "Being satisfied with the colors is the most challenging part of hooking any rug," she said. "I went back to the dye pot many, many times for this rug."

Shawn tries to incorporate a new technique or element into each rug she creates. "This was the first time to have a hit-and-miss area," she said. "I loved doing it but quickly realized that it's not as random as it appears at first glance." Her favorite part of the rug is the bumblebees because they add whimsy and tie the various areas of the rug together.

BEElieve, 35" x 35", #6-cut new and reclaimed wool on monk's cloth. Designed and hooked by Shawn Niemeyer, Centennial, Colorado, 2012.

In the Judges' Words

- Good balance of color and design
- Love the busy bee trail
- Good depth in sunflowers
- Fantastic workmanship

SHAWN NIEMEYER
CENTENNIAL, COLORADO

Shawn had the chance to learn rug hooking 15 years ago, but decided to wait until her children were older and funds weren't so tight. In 2008 she took a class from Debbie McIntosh and has hooked 13 projects in the past 5 years. She is a member of ATHA. This is her first rug to be featured in Celebration.

Contemplation

J udy Cole took one giant step outside her comfort zone when she decided to create this rug. An exhibit of nude rugs planned for a local art gallery spurred her to bare all and pose for photographs that she would then use to hook a nude self-portrait. "Thank goodness for digital cameras!" she said.

After several attempts to hook a realistic rendition of her photo, Judy became frustrated. She found inspiration in a stone sculpture done by a local artist. The result was a body covered in wavy and circular pastel patterns. "Once I listened to my heart, the rug was a joy to hook," she said. "I completed the rug in less than five months."

Judy had to put some extra thought into the highlights and shadows of the body. To make the patterning work, she took some artistic liberties with the placement of the geometric shapes and the designs. She frequently compared her rug to the spotlighted nude photo, evaluating her work to make sure that it remained true to the proportions of her figure. The wandering lines in the light from the spotlight provide a sharp contrast to the directional hooking of the body, making the nude figure stand out against the spotlit background.

Judy spot dyed wool to supplement the fabric she already had in her stash. "Much of the creativity and fun of hooking is hunting for just the right wool," she said.

Judy finished the rug with a crocheted border in a #8-cut wool strip. "The absence of a border was intentional to allow the central design to really stand out," she said.

Contemplation now hangs in Judy's living room.

JUDY COLE
SHELBURNE, VERMONT

A local evening class for beginning rug hookers started Judy on a 4-year, 40-rug exploration of rug hooking. She started with commercially designed primitive patterns and has now progressed to originals with bright colors. Judy is a member of the Green Mountain Rug Guild. This is her second rug to be chosen for Celebration.

Contemplation, 44″ x 49″, #5-, 6-, and 8-cut as-is and overdyed wool on linen. Designed and hooked by Judy Cole, Shelburne, Vermont, 2012. PHOTO BY ANNE-MARIE LITTENBERG

- *Geometric skin? It works!*
- *Blue light and lines effective*
- *Geometric fill adds interest*
- *Shadows create depth*

Doorways of Yarmouth

Specially chosen photographs of doorways capture the unique elements of a small town and county. The Carpetbaggers, a rug hooking group whose president is Shirley Bradshaw, decided to adapt that idea to rug hooking to celebrate the 250th anniversary of Yarmouth, a town in Nova Scotia on the shores of the Atlantic Ocean. The Carpetbaggers invited members of the Rugg Bees, a second local group, to assist in the project.

The rug hookers designed the piece to highlight twenty-four doorways—not just doors. "Doorways were chosen as they reflect the entry into the lives of many people," she said. "Private doorways were intermingled with doorways of historical and government buildings."

Many of the vignettes are simply doors. Others, however, break the typical pattern of showing just an isolated doorway. "Yarmouth is often referred to as a doorway to the province. The ferry Bluenose represents one of the main entries to Nova Scotia," she said. "The milk truck was a well-known delivery service to homes and businesses in the area until very recent years."

Because the piece was designed to be a historical record, each artist color planned her doorway to match the colors of the actual doorways in town. The blue background represents the sea. The lighthouse at the top marks the historic entryway into the town. The red and gold arch at the top of the rug pulls all the colors together.

Vignettes were laid out randomly on a background that is itself two large rectangular doors. Each was balanced by color as much as possible. All smaller doorways are the same size; the large ones were doubled to accommodate the subject. A subtle decoration in the blue background runs from the bottom to the top of the doors. The 24 vignettes were hooked by 25 artists; many more helped with the background and finishing.

The finished piece was shown throughout Yarmouth town and county over the course of a year. It now hangs in a large shadowbox in the foyer of Yarmouth's town hall.

SHIRLEY BRADSHAW
YARMOUTH, NOVA SCOTIA

Shirley Bradshaw has been hooking rugs and attending camps and workshops for 22 years. The Carpetbaggers have been hooking together since 1980. Members of their group range in age from 10 to 92. Individually, they have hooked thousands of pieces and enjoy many styles and techniques. As a group, they have completed 6 rugs for fundraisers or charity.

Doorways of Yarmouth, 48" x 73", #3- and 4-cut wool on linen.
Designed and hooked by Rug Hookers of Yarmouth, Nova Scotia, 2011. PHOTO BY SUE HUTCHINS

Dylan's Bike

Carol Koerner chose this design because of the large headlight and metallic parts of the motorcycle. "I love the challenge of hooking bright, shiny surfaces," she said. "Of course, the fact that this is my handsome grandson didn't hurt either."

In order to keep the emphasis on her grandson and the bike—which he had just bought and was telling her about how he was going to fix it up as she snapped the picture—Carol simplified the original photo. She removed the surrounding clutter in the garage and eliminated the garage door windows from the final pattern.

Carol did her own color planning for this rug, making adjustments along the way. In this piece, she had to overdye the blue she had chosen for the jeans, because the shade she had picked proved to be too bright next to the dull T-shirt and orange of the turn signal.

Finding just the right color for the background, which Carol thought would be an easy task, became a time-consuming chore. "Everything else was done and I realized that the white garage door, which would recede to shades of gray in the background, could not be hooked in that color," she said. "It would kill the whole piece." After sorting through dozens of tans, she visited a home improvement store and picked up a handful of paint chips. When she found just the right shade, she duplicated it in her dye pot.

Carol's favorite part of the rug is "the big shiny headlight. It was the challenge I gave myself, and I believe I managed to capture all the reflections in the faceted glass," she said. To duplicate the shine, Carol used new, pure white wool, ". . . as white as I could find."

The finished rug hangs in the guest bedroom where Dylan stays when he comes to visit.

In the Judges' Words

- *Face excellent*
- *Good shine on metal and glass*
- *Details captured right into the rug*
- *Light bulb reflection well done*

CAROL KOERNER
BETHESDA, MARYLAND

Carol never meant to become a rug hooker, but after taking classes with her mother (who later traded singing and pottery making for rug hooking), she couldn't walk away. Carol has hooked 38 rugs in the past 17 years. Dylan's Bike is her ninth rug to be featured in Celebration.

Dylan's Bike, 23″ x 28″, #3-cut wool on linen.
Designed and hooked by Carol Koerner, Bethesda, Maryland, 2012.

Emma Lou and Grace Go to School

Lynn Ruedger took on the role of storyteller as she designed and color planned this rug to illustrate a story that her rug hooking teacher, Emma Lou Lais, told during workshops. "This story stuck with me and I could easily visualize her as a little girl on her way to school when her horse, Grace, decided to sit down," Lynn recounted. "Her father eventually came to the rescue because no amount of her coaxing could get that horse to move!"

Lynn color planned the rug using wool she had on hand. She pulled leftover 8-value swatches and odds and ends from dye experiments and other projects. Then, she spot dyed greens for the hill and dyed an 8-value swatch for the sky. To give the clouds more dimension, she hooked white mohair yarn in with new and recycled wool.

Lynn enjoys hooking in what she calls "a painterly style" with various cuts, and that preference shows in the many colors that she used throughout the rug. "Grace the horse is my favorite part," she said. "I loved getting the expression right and using bits of unexpected color, such as reds and purples, in her."

To create the illusion of depth in the background, Lynn found herself studying distant horizons wherever she went. "I paid particular attention to how color appeared when it receded," she said, "and I especially took note of where sky met earth. This rug was not meant to be a realistic representation, but more of an 'impressionistic' one."

Lynn worked on the rug for over a year in between camps and workshop projects. *Emma Lou and Grace Go to School* was the last rug she was able to share with her mentor, as Emma Lou has passed away this year.

In the Judges' Words

- *Cute idea*
- *Lovely mix of colors, lavenders, and hi-chroma*
- *The attitude shines through*

LYNN RUEDGER
STEGER, ILLINOIS

Lynn has always enjoyed working with fiber, so her interest in hand-hooked rugs came as no surprise. Since 2000 she has hooked 32 rugs and an unknown number of smaller table mats, artist trading cards, pillows, and ornaments. This is her third rug to be featured in Celebration.

Emma Lou and Grace Go to School, 24″ x 19″, #3- and 4-cut wool and mohair yarn on verel backing.
Designed and hooked by Lynn Ruedger, Steger, Illinois, 2012. PHOTO BY GORDON RUEDGER

Endurance

apri Boyle Jones developed this design for the special exhibit, *Celebration of Life*, at Quayside Art Gallery to honor survivors, remember family and friends, and support caregivers involved in all types of cancers. The worn shoes convey life to be lived by some, a life well lived by those who no longer walk, and the life of caregivers who come forward with a desire to love and help. "Persons persevere every day to gain strength of life, implement preventative measures, and educate with the hope of a cure for the various cancers," she said.

Capri used new and recycled wool for this project. She routinely dyes wool in a variety of techniques and colors to inventory fabric for future use. She estimates that approximately 70 percent of this rug was developed using wools left over from previous projects.

The shoelaces proved to be the most challenging part of this rug. "The shoelaces against the shoes and against the light shining on the floor required thoughtful effort to maintain each element," Capri said. "Subtly using the concept of negative space with the shoelaces aided the correct visual with the whites and lights. I spent a lot of time intently evaluating the white areas."

Capri couldn't identify one part of this rug she liked the best; instead, she said finishing the rug gave her the most joy. "The objective of the project was to increase awareness in the community and assistance for those in need of services," she said. "Most all of us have been touched by this disease—self, family, and/or friends."

Capri whipped the edges with wool yarn to match the adjacent hooked areas. *Endurance* is currently traveling on exhibit at various locations. Upon its sale, 100 percent of the proceeds will be donated to the American Cancer Society.

In the Judges' Words

- *Subtle color*
- *Interesting idea*
- *Good depth*
- *Super use of values*

CAPRI BOYLE JONES
NAVARRE, FLORIDA

Capri learned rug hooking in the hope of making hand-hooked rugs for her floors. In the past 21 years she has hooked more than 250 rugs, decorations, and accessories. She is a member of ATHA and Pearl K. McGown Hookrafters and owns Capri Boyle Rug Studio. This rug is her fourth to appear in Celebration.

Endurance, 24″ x 16″, #3- to 8-cut wool on linen.
Designed and hooked by Capri Boyle Jones, Navarre, Florida, 2012.

Fantasy Painting

for a typical wall hanging. In the upper right hand corner, a hummingbird flies in to gather nectar from a lily. To the upper left, a butterfly flutters out of the picture frame. A bluebird rests on the bottom right edge of the frame. Up and down each side, flowers spill out of the frame. "I thought it would be fun to design a formal floral painting with a very ornate frame and then make it whimsical," he said.

John's rug hooking teacher color planned the rug for him and chose the dye formulas. She coached John to stir the wool almost constantly during the dyeing process to achieve very smooth, even results. He used new white Dorr wool rather than natural for more vibrant and true colors. Red metallic embroidery thread adds iridescence to the hummingbird's throat.

The most challenging part of the rug was shading the frame and the scrolls. "I studied actual carved picture frames to see where the highlights and shadows were," John said. His biggest lesson learned: ". . . patience. I kept looking for ways to improve what I had hooked. Persistence paid off."

John finished the rug with black binding tape and plans to display it in his home.

In the Judges' Words

- *Lovely idea*
- *Fun fantasy*
- *Good shading and depth*
- *Love the elements extending onto the frame*

John L. Leonard almost had a disaster in the making of his rug, *Fantasy Painting*. Fortunately his love of dyeing wool and his attention to detail came to his rescue. "I realized I did not have enough wool of some of the values to complete the frame," he said. "Luckily, I had saved the leftover dyes, so by adding more dye to the lighter values, I was able to produce the values I needed."

John's *trompe l'oeil* (fool the eye) design starts with a colorful still life of a vase full of flowers, but the viewer quickly realizes that this composition has too much action

JOHN L. LEONARD
WILMINGTON, NORTH CAROLINA

John became intrigued with rug hooking when he saw a vintage postcard showing a man hooking a rug. In the past 12 years he has hooked 27 rugs—and also gotten his wife interested in rug hooking. He creates patterns for House of Price and is a member of the Cape Fear Rug Hookers. Fantasy Painting is his first rug to appear in Celebration.

Fantasy Painting, 36" x 41½", #3-cut wool and embroidery thread on rug warp.
Designed and hooked by John L. Leonard, Wilmington, North Carolina, 2012. PHOTO BY MATT BORN

Gallosplace

Teresa started this rug in a workshop and chose some major background colors with Jane Halliwell Green. As for the other colors, "I like to think God planned them," she said. She used photographs and advice from rug hooking friends, but "ultimately I had to trust my eye. I was amazed how something I picked for one area ended up working better in another. The colors did unexpected things when I put them next to each other, and I never seemed to have enough different colors." To keep them all straight, Teresa's mom bought her a fishing tackle box with a multitude of compartments to separate and carry bits of wool. She used spot dyes, casserole dyes, "flat" colors, and plaids.

Her biggest challenge in completing this rug was time. Small cuts and limited time to work on the rug meant that this project took almost three years to complete. "Once the overall design was in my mind, I had to concentrate on building up each unique object," she said. "A square inch or two on a tree was actual progress."

Teresa refers to the finished rug as her "chalk picture," referring to how Mary Poppins turned chalk pictures into real places that she and Bert could visit. "When I worked on this rug, and when I look at it now, I feel myself transported," she said. "It feels like there was a bit of magic involved."

Teresa's husband is custom-making a frame from weathered barn wood, so Teresa finished the rug with a simple hooked beauty line. The framed rug will hang in a guest room and be rotated to the living room wall during the fall season.

One of the perks Teresa Matheny's mother promised when she introduced her daughter to rug hooking was "license to take any wool from her stash." Teresa made use of that promise when she hooked *Gallosplace*, an old farm that her family has used as a weekend country place and reunion spot. "I wanted to commemorate it in my favorite season—autumn—because I love the colors," she said. "My mom hooked a New England fall scene some years earlier. I was itching to get my hands on her beautiful leftovers!"

In the Judges' Words

- *Wonderful balance of buildings and color*
- *One can almost feel the leaves falling*
- *Great use of texture*

TERESA MATHENY
COLUMBIA, MISSOURI

Teresa's mother paved the way for her to learn rug hooking, which gave them some special time together. But in the past seven years, she has yet to hook a rug per se: she has hooked three wall hangings, two pillows, a footstool cover, mug rugs, flowers for hats, and a tree skirt. Gallosplace is her first rug to be featured in Celebration.

Gallosplace, 26¹/₂″ x 18″, #3-, 4-, and 5-cut wool on rug warp.
Designed and hooked by Teresa Matheny, Columbia, Missouri, 2012.

Ghost Horse

Janice Lee drew this design in memory of her horse Blackie. As some black horses will do, Blackie turned gray over time. "I had him through most of the important parts of my life," she said, "but he died at 31 years of age of a stroke with me holding his head in my lap. He is buried by his favorite pasture, under a tree in sight of my front door. Even though he died 12 years ago, I think of him daily. And every once in a while, I catch myself looking twice, because I think I may have caught a glimpse of him."

Janice decided to hook a winter scene of Blackie's favorite pasture with his spirit standing among the trees, but her teacher, Diane Stoffel, had a different idea. "No, that horse is going to be running through those trees," she said. "And when he passes by the tree, he will change the color of the bark."

Janice started the rug during Diane's three-day class, sharing the stories of her and Blackie with her classmates, and then finished the rug in two weeks. She used all wool and overdyed every piece with either pot or spot dyeing. "The whites of the snow and the whites of the sky had to be similar yet different," she said. "And the sky needed to get colder the farther away it was from the ground. I dyed lots of whites—blue whites, gray whites, pink whites, yellow whites—to have the variety I needed."

Hooking the horse's face into the trunk of the tree was the most difficult element of this rug. "But I like that you really have to look close to see it. Like it is a secret," she said.

Janice finished the rug with binding tape and Ryegarn yarn dyed a raisin color to match the border and the purplish/raisin-colored trees. It is on display in Janice's store, Black Horse Antiques.

JANICE LEE
VALLEY, NEBRASKA

When Janice's friend wanted to learn rug hooking and needed two more people in order to keep the class from being cancelled, Janice signed up too—despite having no desire to learn rug hooking herself. Since then, she's hooked 250 rugs. Ghost Horse marks her first rug to appear in Celebration.

In the Judges' Words

- *Beautiful use of neutrals*
- *Neat idea well done*
- *Good balance*
- *Extremely creative*

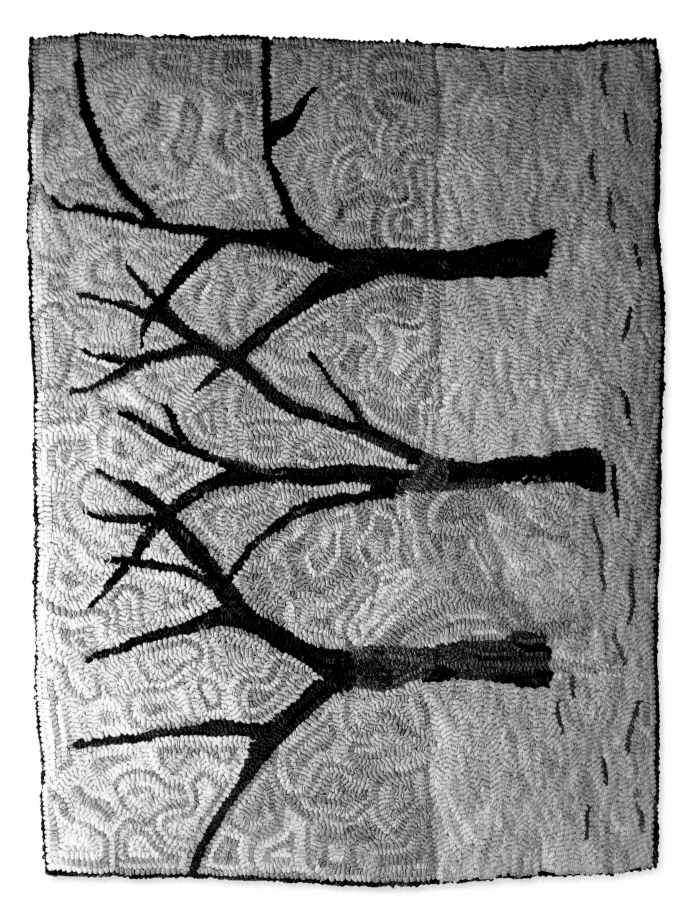

Ghost Horse, 36" x 27", #8-cut wool.
Designed and hooked by Janice Lee, Valley, Nebraska, 2012. PHOTO BY SCOTT AVERY

Guarding Marina

Michele Micarelli is often identified with mermaids because she collects shells and enjoys swimming, but in the past twenty-plus years of rug hooking she has never attempted to hook one.

For this composition, Michele chose a warrior mermaid who is charged with guarding the ocean while she in turn is guarded by her sea monster muse.

Michele planned the colors for this rug, opting for the rich blues and greens of the ocean and the kelp lair in which the mermaid is placed. She used new and recycled wool as well as some alternate fabrics and beading. The beading is most apparent in the mermaid's headdress. Michelle chose a variety of beads for the symmetrical head-dress and topped it off with a small painted shell. The beads and shell are repeated in the mermaid's necklace.

The entire rug proved to be a study in contrasts. Her favorite part of the rug is the mermaid's scales. "The scales have the look I was going for—I was trying to make her look fishlike," she said. "I think the detail and contrast is right."

While many areas of the rug stand out for their combination of colors, the section that catches the viewer's eye first is the mermaid's hair. From a distance, the wide variety of colors work together, but up close the viewer can see just how many colors were used in that small space. Their placement may appear random, but it's not: certain colors, like the bright yellows, act as highlights while others are used as the mid-tones and shadows (purples).

Contrast also plays an important part in the water and the kelp, which go from light to dark as the viewer's eye travels from the base and foreground to the top and background of the hooked piece.

In the Judges' Words

- *Fantastic design and execution*
- *Beautiful scales, seaweed, and hair*
- *Good depth in water*
- *Super attention to detail*

MICHELE MICARELLI
NEW HAVEN, CONNECTICUT

Michele is a bead artist and doll maker as well as a rug hooking artist and teacher. She belongs to several rug hooking groups and has served on the board of ATHA. Her rugs have been featured in a number of publications, including Celebration.

Guarding Marina, 38″ x 68″, #2-, 3-, 4-, and 5-cut wool, yarn, and beads on linen.
Designed and hooked by Michele Micarelli, New Haven, Connecticut, 2012. PHOTO BY ANNE-MARIE LITTENBERG

I Wish

Brigitte Webb likens rug hooking to reading a good book: you can't put it down, and you don't know the end until you're finished. Her garden pictorial, *I Wish*, fits perfectly into that description.

Brigitte, a self-described "compulsive rug hooker," started *I Wish* by drawing only the outline for the finished size and nothing else. "Then, against recognized convention," she said, "I just started to hook at the bottom middle of the rug and built up the design from there using shapes, textures, and colours that I felt complemented each other. The garden grew out of my mind and onto the backing."

The wool for this rug came as gifts from hooking friends. Brigitte received some spot dyes, mottled dyes, and casserole dyes that she used in the design. She purchased some new Dorr wool and incorporated some handspun yarns with metallic thread woven into the strands. "Those reminded me of drops of dew on flowers in the early morning," she said.

The most challenging aspect of hooking this rug was to create the feeling of being in a garden. "I love flowers and gardens and the wonderful array of colours that sit happily beside one another," she said. Brigitte pulled from memories of her favorite gardens and hooked one that showed a profusion of flowers. The shrubs and stone wall in the background added to the feeling of being isolated from the outside world, surrounded by blossoms.

Brigitte whipped the edges of the rug with multicolored handspun wool yarn that picks up the oranges, yellows, blues, and reds of the flowers in the foreground. The finished rug hangs in her living room—out of direct sunlight—where it brightens the room even on the gloomiest days.

In the Judges' Words

- *Good depth*
- *Flowers well mixed*
- *Love the colorful whipped edges*
- *Nice stone wall*

BRIGITTE WEBB
DINGWALL, UNITED KINGDOM

Brigitte started rug hooking when her son fell in love with a girl whose mother was the director of a rug hooking group. Since 2006 she's hooked more than 80 mats from no bigger than her hand to a 7-foot floor rug. I Wish is her first rug to be featured in Celebration.

I Wish, 23¹/₂″ x 18″, #3-, 4-, and 5-cut wool, yarn, and silk on monk's cloth.
Designed and hooked by Brigitte Webb, Dingwall, United Kingdom, 2012. PHOTO BY SEORIS N. MCGILLIVRAY

In the Woods Abstract

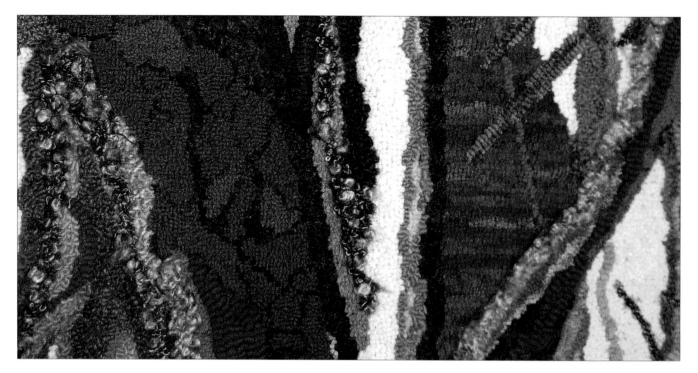

Gunda Gamble enjoys designing pieces that incorporate landscapes, impressionism, and abstracts. Her rug, *In the Woods Abstract*, was inspired by tree bark. She drew a few starting lines on rug warp and created this freeform abstract from there.

Gunda does her own dyeing and used a variety of dye techniques—including spot, marble, casserole, and value dyeing. She chose the colors to keep the overall feel of the rug warm and earthy, like the bark she was trying to imitate.

To keep the abstract feel of the piece without losing the feel of the original bark, Gunda used both new and recycled wool. "I used swatches and noodles (worms) left over from previous projects and added some fun and fancy yarns I found in my knitting stash," she said.

More than anything else, Gunda found the size of this rug to be a challenge. The finished piece measures 40" wide and 69" high. "The hardest part of this project was the color and fabric selection," she said. "I had to repeatedly put it on the floor, stand back, and view it in its entirety."

Gunda also found that rug warp gets very heavy when working with such a large rug. "I found it frustrating that my gripper strips on my frame were frequently pulling my yarns back out as I removed and replaced my piece," she said.

Gunda whipped the edges and then built a wooden frame upon which the rug could be mounted. The completed piece hangs on the wall in her great room above the main staircase.

In the Judges' Words

- *Movement and flow of color and light evoke the shifting shadow of the woods*
- *Good color abstract*
- *Enormous variety for one subject matter*

GUNDA GAMBLE
BRESLAU, ONTARIO

Gunda became interested in rug hooking when she joined a crafting group and saw some of the other members rug hooking. She took a beginner's workshop in 2004 and has completed 30 pieces, mostly large. She is a member of the Ontario Hooking Craft Guild. This rug is her first to appear in Celebration.

In the Woods Abstract, 40" x 69", #3- to 8-cut wool and fancy yarn on rug warp.
Designed and hooked by Gunda Gamble, Breslau, Ontario, 2012.

My First Love

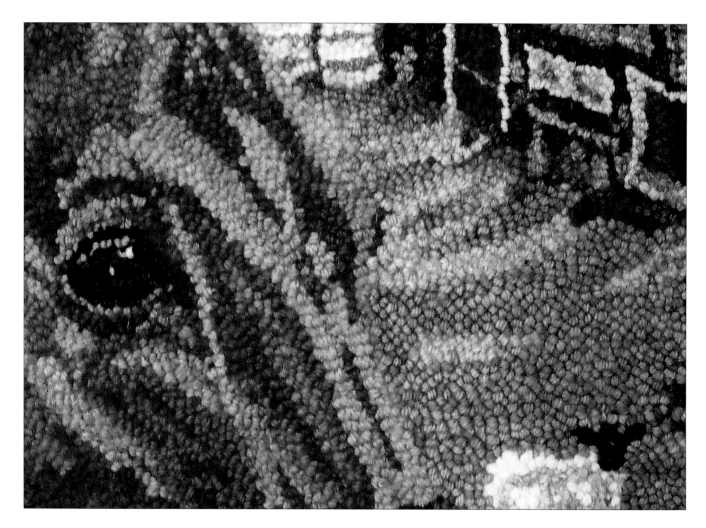

Sometimes, when you love something so much, hooking it just right can be an almost insurmountable challenge. Simone Vojvodin found herself in that very spot when she decided to hook a portrait of her first true love: Sparky, a chestnut gelding.

Simone knew she wanted Sparky to be the prominent figure in her rug's design, and she wanted to include other memories from her time with her beloved horse. She added the barn where a hay loft became her bedroom for a summer; the chickens that her family raised; Beau, a sheep that had been an actress in a Shakespeare play; and Louise, her best friend's horse. "All these precious memories and many more are wrapped up in a pretty country scene," she said.

Simone stopped and started often, putting the rug down when she needed to think about the next step or when other projects intervened. Getting started on Sparky, how-ever, impeded her progress the most. "I really wanted to get him just right, and at first I struggled with it," she said. "When I came back to it months later, it just flowed."

Whipping the edges was another challenge. Simone taught herself the herringbone stitch and then used it to cover a thick cord. The cord starts within the rug as the horse's halter and then surrounds the rest of the rug, ending with a tassel at the base. Her attention to detail as she punch hooked the rug, combined with the unique edge, make this rug reversible.

Simone dip dyed 4-ply heavyweight wool rug yarn for the sky and the smaller horse, and overdyed commercially dyed rug yarn for Sparky. She spot dyed all the other rug yarn with various color combinations. The finished rug hangs on her dining room wall.

My First Love, 34" x 32¹/₂", 4-ply wool rug yarn on monk's cloth. Designed and hooked by Simone Vojvodin, Parkhill, Ontario, 2012.

In the Judges' Words

- *Very fun finish*
- *Great depth and highlights*
- *Beautiful horse*
- *Fine finishing*

SIMONE VOJVODIN
PARKHILL, ONTARIO

Simone started punch hooking rugs soon after she saw Celebration *at her local library. In the past five years she's completed an uncountable number of rugs. Simone is a certified Oxford Punch Needle instructor and runs Red Maple Ruggery.* My First Love *is her second rug to be featured in* Celebration.

Seasons

Sara Beth Black puzzled over this design for many years. She always wanted to do a rug that showed not just the four seasons, but the transitions between the seasons as well. The answer came with a little bit of help from rug hooking teacher Diane Stoffel: each tree would show the beginning of the season on the left side and the full season on the right side.

Sara Beth also struggled with the trees themselves. They are central to the success of her design and she was afraid that regular hooking techniques would leave the trees looking too flat to get the look she wanted. Her solution was to hook the trees in a method called "double stitching," where two colors are pulled at the same time.

The final element of Sara Beth's design was transitioning the ground and the sky into each season. Sara Beth let the trees lead the way in each section and simply transferred whatever season the tree was exhibiting into the ground below and the sky above. The center of the rug is a blue that could be shared by all four (or eight, if you count the transitions) seasons.

Sara Beth used a combination of new and recycled 100 percent wool. To get the colors she needed, she used leftovers from her stash and dyed new colors with casseroles, dips, and spots.

The entire rug took about 18 months to finish. She has trouble picking out a favorite part of the rug because the changing of the seasons is actually her favorite season. "I love it all!" she said. "It is exactly what I was trying to create in capturing the seasons in the Blue Ridge Mountains."

Seasons, 40" diameter, #4- to 7-cut hand-dyed wool on linen. Designed and hooked by Sara Beth Black, Arden, North Carolina, 2011. PHOTO BY TIM BARNWELL

SARA BETH BLACK
ARDEN, NORTH CAROLINA

When Sara Beth was a teenager, her job was to pull apart skirts and jackets for her grandmother, who would then cut them and make them into beautiful hand-hooked rugs. When her son was born, she returned to the art form and has been hooking nonstop for 22 years. Seasons is her first rug to appear in Celebration.

In the Judges' Words

- *Good color and execution*
- *Fun motifs*
- *Good use of "double stitching"*
- *Originality is super!*

Solitude

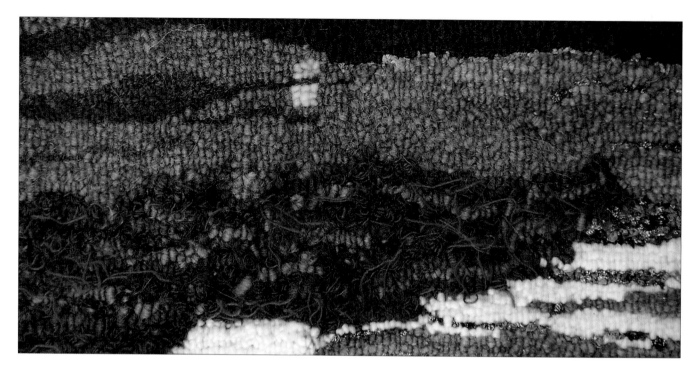

Karen Miller's goal for this rug was to capture the solitude that she, her husband, and young daughter experienced while staying in a house named "Solitude" on the Faroe Islands during a family vacation. "The flat, dark blues of the stormy sky and the lively reds, whites, and greens around our cottage made us feel like we'd been closed off in our own little world," she said. "The three of us felt so safe inside together while the storm raged outside."

Karen hooked this rug entirely from new yarns, including wool yarns, Icelandic lopi yarn, novelty yarns, bamboo yarn, acrylic yarn, and metallic yarn. She did no dyeing, but she included a bit of metallic-accented ribbon to bring more life to the water in contrast to the flat sky.

The core element of *Solitude* is the mood. "While I found that the color selections for the house and the headland were very forgiving, finding just the right blues for the sky and capturing just the right amount of activity in the water to catch the feel of a 'closed-off world' was considerably more subtle." In the end, Karen went with the sky color combinations that felt right.

Karen found the heavy window frame at a salvage yard and knew it was just what she needed to complete the feeling of solitude. She hooked each pane of the rug and installed them separately. "It was challenging to line up all of the lines in the piece, particularly in the house. Through

trial and error and having to rip out a few rows here and there and start again, I eventually got it to work."

The finished piece hangs in the living room of her home, reminding her of the solitude her family felt within the walls of their cottage retreat.

In the Judges' Words

- *I want to open the window and lean out*
- *Love the concept*
- *Feels lonely and damp*
- *Good depth*

KAREN MILLER
OTTAWA, ONTARIO

Karen used to cross-stitch but gave it up for rug hooking when she discovered a small kit in Nova Scotia. Since 2008, she has hooked 31 wall hangings of all shapes and sizes. She is a member of the Green Mountain Rug Hooking Guild and the Ontario Hooking Craft Guild. Solitude *is her first rug to appear in* Celebration.

Solitude, 38¹/₂″ x 21¹/₂″, *wool yarns, novelty yarns, rug warp, antique window frame.*
Designed and hooked by Karen Miller, Ottawa, Ontario, 2012. PHOTO BY DANIEL MACDONALD

Spirit Bear

Lucy Walsh has always been intrigued by Native American culture and design. The idea for her rug, *Spirit Bear*, gelled after she read about the Kermode bears—sometimes called *spirit bears* or ghost bears—found on the coastal islands off British Columbia.

Kermode bears, she learned, are a subspecies of the American black bear. About 10 percent of the black bear population has completely white-colored fur. According to Native American legend, the master of the universe created one white bear for every ten black bears as a reminder of the hardships during the ice age. They also symbolize peace and harmony, which she tried to capture in her design.

In addition to the Kermode bear, Lucy worked a handful of Native American symbols into the orange background of the rug: a turtle, a snake, a fish, mountains, the sun, and a pine tree. The eagle is a symbol of protection and the blue and yellow border colors represent the sun and sky. The black border features a Bear Paw quilt pattern and a Native American beadwork motif.

Lucy found that the most difficult part of this rug was binding the edge. She chose a black, leather-looking, slightly stretchy fabric that reminded her of the textured look of a bear's nose. She machine stitched the backing to the edge of the hooking, allowed the material to extend 1/2" beyond the loops, then folded it under for a 3" hand-stitched hem on the back of the rug.

The completed rug takes its place among the rugs that Lucy rotates throughout her house. All of her rugs have seen service on tabletops, walls, floors, and rolled up in a copper apple butter kettle. "If things you love are incorporated in an original design, the rug really becomes an extension of you and your vision . . . they are a part of your story," she said.

In the Judges' Words

- *Good primitive interpretation*
- *Good balance of color*
- *It is a puzzle; symbols are fun to find*
- *Color plan coordinates well with design*

LUCY WALSH
UNION GAP VILLAGE, NEW JERSEY

Lucy has admired hooked rugs ever since her mother took up rug hooking at an adult education class, but found it too tedious to pursue until 1990. Since then she has hooked more than 40 rugs. All her rugs are hooked in a primitive style. Spirit Bear is her first rug to be featured in Celebration.

Spirit Bear, 29″ x 19″, #6-cut new and recycled wool on linen.
Designed and hooked by Lucy Walsh, Union Gap Village, New Jersey, 2011.

The Purple House

Diane Ayles tells us that she created *The Purple House* during a special time in her life. "This is a special time for me—a time when I can express my love of nature and share it with people." Her *Celebration* entry, *The Purple House*, is a statement of her approach to her artwork.

Diane was commissioned to hook *The Purple House* by a friend. A unique landmark in the area, this purple-encased home is now a popular ice cream parlor, its steps and porch a gathering place for people during the summer.

To capture the rich colors of the house and the contrasting colors of the trees and the nearby flowers, Diane dyed her own wool. She combined a range of dyeing processes, from spot to dip to casserole, to bring this piece to life. "Through careful studying and blending of many colours, I recreated the house's true colours," she said. "Each piece of dyed wool adds a special touch."

The many shades of green foliage that surround the house give the composition depth and interest and keep the focus of the rug on the structure of the house. Diane hooked darker greens above the house and to the right to make those areas recede; brighter greens and a splash of yellow bring the viewer's eye forward.

Diane used 100 percent wool with a little bit of silk, lamb's locks, and a few textured wools. She completed the rug in just over four months, noting no particular challenges. "I believe I have a natural gift for creating colours and love expressing what I see," she said. "I reach a point where the work becomes a part of me."

The rug was professionally framed and is now privately owned.

In the Judges' Words

- Great use of shadows to create the soul of the house
- Great sky reflection in the windows
- Fantastic foliage
- Good color and execution

DIANE AYLES
HUNTSVILLE, ONTARIO

Diane is a self-taught artist. She learned rug hooking, along with crocheting, knitting, embroidery, and other handcrafts, from her mother, and her father encouraged her to pursue her artistic talents. Diane has hooked 13 rugs and is a member of the Ontario Rug Hooking Guild. This is her first Celebration rug.

The Purple House, 37¹/₂" x 23", #3-cut hand-dyed wool on rug warp.
Designed and hooked by Diane Ayles, Huntsville, Ontario, 2011.

Toronto Graffiti

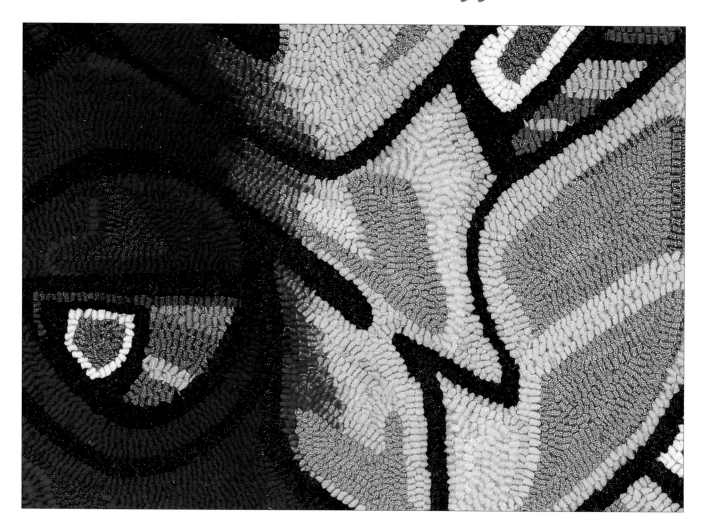

Kathryn Taylor found inspiration for this series of rugs all around her as she traveled. "I recognize that graffiti is not considered by some to be an art at all. In fact, many view it as vandalism," she said. "I see graffiti as a transient art form."

Kathryn combined her two loves, photography and rug hooking, in this project. As she found graffiti in her travels, she photographed it and then used her photographs to design and color plan a rug. "The colours were a given because the designs were based on my photographs; however, when I selected the fabrics, I was as mindful of the colour values as the colours themselves," she said.

Thrift shops became Kathryn's go-to spot for the recycled fabrics that she used in her rugs. She searched for fabrics that were at least 70 percent wool and overdyed them as needed. "Because I wanted the whites to be bright, I did purchase some Dorr white (not natural) wool," she said, "which worked well."

The research and design phases were Kathryn's most challenging aspects of this rug series. "There was an element of risk because I didn't know, until all nine parts were hung on the wall, that the concept would even work," she said. The entire series took a year to complete. "The time invested was substantial, so I had to remain focused on completing all nine parts."

Kathryn learned a lot from working on this rug, and not just about designing and rug hooking. "I learned that the canvas, be it a fence, a wall, an overpass, or a piece of linen, is, after all, just another canvas," she said. "I particularly enjoy the fact that my kids (in their twenties) are engaged and interested in what can be achieved with a traditional craft."

Toronto Graffiti, 9 pieces, each 14", #6-cut wool on linen.
Designed and hooked by Kathryn Taylor, Toronto, Ontario, 2012.

In the Judges' Words

- *Gives me a whole new appreciation for graffiti*
- *Interesting presentation*
- *Unique subject matter*
- *Great color and design*

KATHRYN TAYLOR
TORONTO, ONTARIO

Kathryn learned rug hooking from Barb D'Arcy and hooked her first rug in 1996, but she didn't hook her second rug until 2006. Since then she's hooked seven more rugs. Kathryn belongs to the Ontario Hooking Craft Guild. This is her first rug to be featured in Celebration.

Waiting for Leftovers

Grace E. Collette captures designs that make people smile. "I wanted viewers of this rug to feel the animals surrounding them in the forest at night, the warmth of the campfire, and the love of a father and son.

Grace planned all the colors, basing them on what she would see, not on what she would know. "For example," she said, "I made the front of my grandson's dungarees orange, as a reflection of the firelight, although I know dungarees are blue; I added black, yellow, and blue to the green tree; and I made a blue and black raccoon, as it might appear in the woods on a moonlit night."

Grace used a variety of wool, plus gold Christmas ribbon and variegated yarn in this piece. She found dyeing the wool for the fire to be the most difficult part of her color planning. "I wanted swatches to transition from white to yellow to orange to red to maroon to fuchsia—14 different pieces of wool in all." She used the jar dyeing method to get the exact colors and transitions she needed.

To get the positioning of her son and grandson correct, Grace took pictures of the two sitting on her sofa then used the pictures as reference. She paid close attention to their faces but changed their clothes to make a stronger focal point.

Grace enjoyed hooking every part of the rug but notes that her favorite part is the final composition. "I like how it transmits the feelings that I wanted it to while maintaining balance, a strong focal point, contiguous value masses, perspective, drama, a limited color palette, and the circular plan that keeps the viewer's eye moving within the piece," she said.

The finished rug will be a gift to her son and grandson.

In the Judges' Words

- *Wonderful concept*
- *Good fire and firelight surrounding it*
- *Wonderful story rug*
- *Finishing is top notch*

GRACE E. COLLETTE
RAYMOND, NEW HAMPSHIRE

Grace took her first lessons in rug hooking 40-some years ago from Ruth Hall at a local YWCA, but then had to wait another 35 years to really get started. In the past five years she has completed seven rugs. Grace belongs to several rug hooking guilds. Waiting for Leftovers is her third rug to appear in Celebration.

Waiting for Leftovers, 34″ x 24″, #3-cut wool on linen.
Designed and hooked by Grace Collette, Raymond, New Hampshire, 2012.

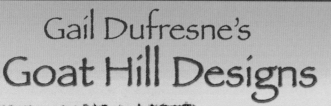

Dear Celebration Reader:

Which rugs are your favorites?

The judges have chosen the finalists—now it is up to you to tell us which of these rugs deserve the honor of being named Readers' Choice winners.

Review each of the winning rugs carefully and make your selections—1st, 2nd, and 3rd choice for each of the Commercial, Original, Adaptation, and Primitive categories. Mark your choices on the attached ballot and be sure to mail it in before December 31, 2013.

Or vote online. Go to *www.rughooking magazine.com*, and look for the *Celebration* Readers' Choice link.

RHM appreciates the time you take to send in your Readers' Choice vote. Please help us honor the rug hooking artists represented within the pages of *Celebration XXIII* by voting for your choice of the best of the best.

Sincerely,

Debra Smith

Editor

READERS' CHOICE BALLOT

After reviewing all the rugs, fill out this ballot and mail it in to vote (Canadians, please use an envelope and your own postage). The winners of the Readers' Choice Contest will be announced in the June/July/August 2014 issue of *Rug Hooking* magazine. **Note: Ballots must be received by December 31, 2013.**

ORIGINAL RUG	ADAPTATIONS
1ST CHOICE	1ST CHOICE
2ND CHOICE	2ND CHOICE
3RD CHOICE	3RD CHOICE
COMMERCIAL RUG	PRIMITIVE
1ST CHOICE	1ST CHOICE
2ND CHOICE	2ND CHOICE
3RD CHOICE	3RD CHOICE

NAME

ADDRESS

CITY/STATE/ZIP   PHONE NUMBER

Never miss an edition of
CELEBRATION OF HAND-HOOKED RUGS
by joining our RHM Book Club

Yes! I want to make sure I never miss an edition of *Celebration of Hand-Hooked Rugs*. Please sign me up for your risk-free RHM Book Club. I understand each time a new **Rug Hooking** book is published it will be automatically shipped to me; this includes our annual edition of *Celebration of Hand-Hooked Rugs*. Each book will be mine to examine for 21 days. If I like what I see, I'll keep the book and pay the invoice. If I'm not delighted, I'll return the book at *Rug Hooking* magazine's expense, and owe nothing.

NAME

ADDRESS

CITY/STATE/ZIP   PHONE NUMBER

E-mail Address

BCEL13

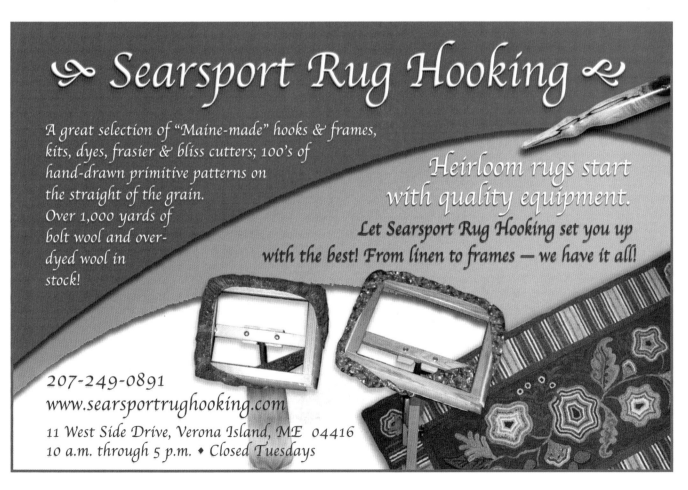

Adam

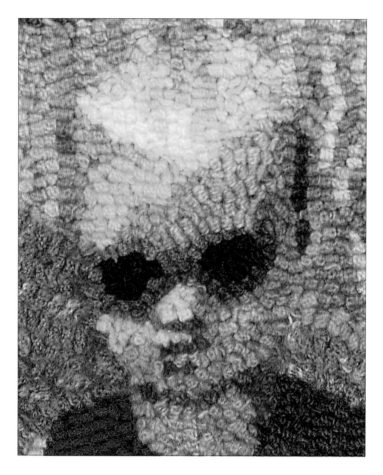

Linda Bell notes that since rug hooking has "taken over her life," she often sees photographs that just call out to be hooked. That was the inspiration behind this rug hooking of her grandson, Adam. Linda's daughter took the picture, and the minute Linda saw it, she knew she needed to hook it.

Linda designed this rug to match the photograph exactly but ended up making several changes as she hooked. The road in the original photograph is much wider and longer; she made it smaller to give more perspective to the portrait and to keep the focus on her grandson. The original photo also shows just greenery along the side of the road; Linda added the pink flowers to the right to add some contrast and interest to the piece.

For this rug, Linda used all new wool and spot dyes created either with the traditional method of spotting wool as it is in the dye pot, or by the Presto Pot method, which makes use of a pot with a spigot attached (a common tool for candle making). "Dyeing my own wool is half the fun," Linda said.

While she likes Adam's swagger and the sunglasses that complete the look, Linda's favorite part of the rug is her grandson's shadow. "As soon as I hooked his shadow, the piece came alive," she said. She knew she had done a good job when Adam took a look at the piece, gave her a big smile, and said, "That's me!"

Linda hooked the piece in several months and then had it professionally framed. Through completing this piece, she learned that it's okay to make changes or additions to a design to make it more artistically pleasing. She found that freeing herself from duplicating the photograph as is allowed her to focus on the true essence of the hooked piece: her grandson's confident stroll along a country road.

In the Judges' Words

- *Good photo interpretation*
- *Good use of color and value to create light and shadow*
- *Great perspective and nice foliage*

Adam, 19″ x 23″, #3-cut wool on linen. Adapted with permission from a photograph by the artist's daughter and hooked by Linda Bell, Hiawassee, Georgia, 2011. PHOTO BY SHAWNTA SHOOK

LINDA BELL
HIAWASSEE, GEORGIA

Linda started rug hooking after she saw a woman demonstrating rug hooking during a home tour. "I literally ran up to her and asked what she was doing and where I could learn." Since then she's hooked about 50 rugs and framed pieces and many more small items, like coasters and flower pins, than she can count. This is her first rug to appear in Celebration.

At the Beach

Gail Ferdinando has always loved this photo of her kids and thought it would be a challenge to recreate it as a hooked rug. And she will be the first to admit that she was right. "All the faces were a huge challenge," she said. "And for some reason, the boys' tee shirts were really a challenge as well."

Gail started hooking this rug at a camp with Diane Stoffel. To help her work through the challenges, Diane had Gail turn the photo and the rug upside down to hook all the faces. "It worked amazingly well," she said. "Later I was having trouble hooking the tee shirts and decided to try her trick of turning the rug and photo upside down, and again it helped tremendously.

Norma Batastini drew the pattern on backing and color planned the rug to match the photo. She also dyed the new and recycled wool that Gail would need. To finish the rug, Gail whipped the edges with wool yarn to match the colors at the edge of the rug. Then she sewed binding tape along the back.

Gail noted, at the risk of offending her boys, that her favorite part of the rug is her daughter in the middle chair. "It just looks like her," she said, "and I really love the colorful chair."

With all the challenges this rug presented, Gail learned a very useful lesson. "I learned that if you are struggling with hooking something realistic from a photo, the best thing to do is to turn everything upside down," Gail said. "It helps you to hook what is actually there, not what you think should be there. And it really works!"

In the Judges' Words

- *The punch of color behind the children and the waves rolling in create a serene scene at the beach.*
- *Love her little top knot*
- *Nice matching edge*
- *I can feel the warmth and hear the waves*

GAIL FERDINANDO
PITTSTOWN, NEW JERSEY

Gail's stepmom put together a small beginner kit for her to try. She finished it by the end of the weekend and went out that day to buy her first pattern. In the past 12 years, she has hooked almost 30 rugs and pillows. At the Beach is her first rug to be featured in Celebration. (Gail's sister Debbie Walsh also has a winning rug in this issue.)

At The Beach, 31″ x 21″, #3-, 4-, and 6-cut wool on linen.
Adapted from a photo and hooked by Gail Ferdinando, Pittstown, New Jersey, 2012.

Autumn Landscape

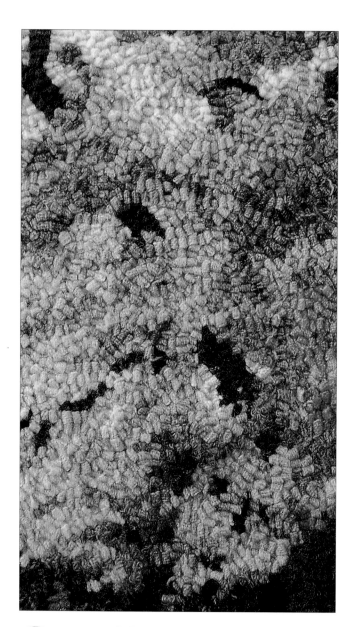

Suzanne color planned the rug to use only wool that was already in her stash. That stash was filled with hand-dyed wool left over from many other projects. Most of it is spot dyed over new wool. A few textures are used in the distant trees and tree trunks.

As Suzanne got started, the leaves quickly became the most challenging aspect of the rug. "Doing the leaves was like putting a puzzle together," she said. "I hooked the high-lights first then the shadows," she said, "then I had to find just the right piece of wool to bring them together."

Once the rug was finished, those challenging leaves were her favorite part. Her goal was to capture the blazing oranges, reds, and yellows of the autumn-clothed trees, a task that she feels she accomplished by focusing on the dark colors in the composition as much as the brights.

She created the grasses from even more bright autumn tones. "I wanted them to appear as individual blades of grass so I hooked them in vertical wavy lines using the colors of the leaves," she said.

Suzanne finished the rug by mounting it on stretchers and placing it in a floating frame.

In the Judges' Words

- *The flaming colors of autumn and shifting light are captured with the use of value*
- *Wonderful use of fall colors*
- *Masterful blend of colors and values*

S uzanne Sandvik enjoys the challenge of making a hooked picture look as real as possible. As an oil painter and pastelist turned rug hooker, it took her a while to understand that wool just doesn't "paint" as well as oils and pastels, but she still has lots of fun trying.

This colorful fall scene gave Suzanne a chance to once again paint with wool. One of her rug hooking students brought in several pieces of her sister's artwork as part of a rug hooking class. Suzanne was immediately enamored with the blazing autumn colors of one painting and decided to recreate the scene as a hooked rug wall hanging.

SUZANNE SANDVIK
BRIGHTON, MICHIGAN

Suzanne was demonstrating basket weaving at an art fair when the rug hooker behind her inadvertently converted her, not with the front of her rug, but with the back. "I was really struck by the beauty of her flowers." She belongs to several rug hooking groups. Autumn Landscape is her first rug to appear in Celebration.

Autumn Landscape, 24" x 18", #4-cut wool on rug warp.
Adapted with permission and hooked by Suzanne Sandvik, Brighton, Michigan, 2012.

Blue-Footed Boobies

Mary Beth Westcott's choice of topics for her rug hooking projects is inspired by her love of animals and nature. *Blue-Footed Boobies* is an adaptation of a photograph that Mary Beth's daughter took when she visited the Galapagos Islands. She found the male birds interesting and was intrigued by their unusual blue feet. "Like other rug hookers, I spend most of my time saying, 'Now that would make a good rug,'" she said. In this case, she was right on track.

Mary Beth took the colors for her hooked rug directly from the photograph and the natural colors of the boobies and the sandy beach. For the background, she added touches of the same colors that she used in the birds but "pepped it up" with some darker blues, purples, and camel colors. She was especially pleased with the slight blue reflection of the birds' feet on their underbellies.

Mary Beth dyed much of the wool herself using the spot dye method and supplemented her stash with spot-dyed wool she purchased at rug camps. She added some textured wool in with the spot-dyed wool for the background—a first!—and was pleasantly surprised with the results.

While Mary Beth admits to never wanting to hook another twig again, she also notes that the twigs are one of her favorite parts of the rug. "When I hook, I love to have a big pile of spot-dyed strips next to me so I can hunt and come up with just the right color for that spot," she said. "Sometimes a strip seems to say 'pick me.' This was especially true when I was hooking the many twigs for the background."

The expressions of the birds in the photograph captured Mary Beth's imagination. As she hooked, she puzzled over their personalities. They were doing a mating dance when the picture was taken, but she is convinced that there seems to be more going on "in those little bird brains." She strived to harness that feeling and hook it into the rug.

In the Judges' Words

- *Great detail on birds*
- *Masterful use of values in a neutral color palette*
- *Love the subtle colors and shading*
- *Nice use of directional hooking*

Blue-Footed Boobies, 25$\frac{1}{2}$" x 28", #2-, 3-, and 4-cut wool on linen. *Adapted with permission from a photograph by Alison Barnes and hooked by Mary Beth Westcott, Gonzales, Texas, 2012.* PHOTO BY CARR IMAGERY

MARY BETH WESTCOTT
GONZALES, TEXAS

Mary Beth taught herself how to hook but then found guidance in her first teacher, Ronnie Roisman. She designs her own rugs, often from her own photographs. Mary Beth is a member of the San Antonio ATHA group, and this rug marks her third piece to be featured in Celebration.

Closing the Bargain

The result is a pictorial that she just adores. "I love every part of this rug," she said.

Sally purchased all the wool for this rug. She chose spot dyes, overdyes, and textures—no plain solid color wool. "The painting is from the 1890s, so it was quite dull," she said. "I brightened it up a bit."

The color variations show clearly in the faded paint on the side of the barn, the rich greens of the grass, and the golds and browns of the haystacks in the background. A mix of colors form the rich colors of the gentlemen's attire, and attention to wrinkles makes their figures even more realistic.

A close-up look at the faces of the men shows Sally's incredible attention to detail. A thin line of hooked loops forms the piece of hay in the farmer's hand, and more lines detail the ears of both men. Noses of the pigs that might be the object of the sale push through the holes in the fence, hoping to reach the basket of corn that the farmer left behind him as he concentrates on the business at hand. Sally is able to capture the story behind the scene based on her in-depth knowledge of life on a farm and masterful hooking skills.

In the Judges' Words

- *Fun story rug*
- *Wonderful detail, great execution*
- *Great depth and use of color*
- *Superb workmanship and finishing*

S ally Hentges fell in love with the painting *Closing the Bargain* the minute she saw it but "really didn't think she could pull off" this rug hooked rendition of the painting. "I grew up on a farm, which I dearly loved," she said. "That was a big part of why I chose to try an adaptation of the painting."

Sally's challenges all related to the difficulty of this piece, and they started as soon as she started hooking and continued through the final loop of the rug. "I love a challenge," she said. "I met it by not giving up."

SALLY HENTGES
DUBUQUE, IOWA

After hearing an advertisement for a rug hooking cutter on a radio station, Sally called and not only bought the cutter, but she also got an invitation to the next meeting of the local rug hooking group. She has hooked 11 projects in the last 13 years. This rug is her first to be featured in Celebration.

Closing the Bargain, 51" x 35", #2-, 3-, and 4-cut wool on linen.
Adapted with permission and hooked by Sally Hentges, Dubuque, Iowa, 2012. PHOTO BY JULIE WINKLER

Dream

A class with Michele Micarelli at the Caraway Rug Camp taught Karen how to "think outside the box" by using various enhancements. "I learned yarn, buttons, ribbon, silks, stockings, beads, sequins, and so on, can add life and excitement to hooked rugs," she said. "It was a wonderful class and opened my mind to trying different things."

Karen applied those techniques in *Dream* in several ways. She hooked two different metallic ribbons along with the tan wool used for the girl's hair, she chose a green/gold oval metallic button for the eye for the large hummingbird, and she sewed Swarovski crystal beads into the background. "My favorite part of this rug is the embellishments," she said. "Adding beads, buttons, and ribbon added new excitement and fun to hooking."

The most challenging aspect of this rug was two-fold: first, capturing the detail and color of the hummingbirds' feathers, and second, determining the right amount and type of embellishment to use. She ended up making a very large enlargement of the greeting card to help with both aspects. "I tried to be very deliberate and patient with the process, and the results were rewarding," she said.

Karen collects ladybug artifacts and includes ladybugs in her hooked rugs. Can you find the ladybug in *Dream*?

In the Judges' Words

- *Great soft tones and execution*
- *Good variation in colors and values*
- *Great color plan*

Karen Whidden enjoys hooking very detailed, colorful, and challenging pieces. She found all three of those elements in this adaptation of Jody Bergsma's greeting card *Dream*. "I liked the soft background colors and dramatic colors of the hummingbirds in the greeting card," she said, "and I decided to try to capture that magic in my rug."

After receiving permission from Jody to recreate her design as a rug hooking, Karen started dyeing wool for the rug. She used Dorr natural 100 percent wool—no plaid, striped, textured, or recycled wool—and ProChem dyes with regular, overdyeing, and spot-dyeing techniques.

KAREN WHIDDEN
SOUTHERN PINES, NORTH CAROLINA

Karen learned to hook rugs when she and her husband retired to Southern Pines in the fall of 2003. Since then she has hooked more than 135 rugs, pillows, mats, and wall hangings. She is a member of McGown, ATHA, and the Sandhills Rug Artists. Dream *is her sixth rug to appear in* Celebration.

Dream, 17" x 23", #3- and 4-cut wool on rug warp. Adapted with permission from an illustration by Jody Bergsma and hooked by Karen Whidden, Southern Pines, North Carolina, 2012.

Easter Sunday

up choosing a blue-green coat for her mother because that had been her favorite color. She chose the other colors of the coats and hats based on balance throughout the rug.

Susan used as-is wool and both new and recycled wool from her stash that she had previously dyed. The only wool that was specifically dyed for this rug was the sky. Susan's mother's coat also has a few bits of velour and silk.

The hats are Susan's favorite part of the rug by far because of their flamboyance and because they divulge a little bit about the personality of each woman. Susan decided to make each woman's hat match the coat she was wearing. The corsages offer a beautiful bit of color, and again, since Susan was working from a black and white photograph, she used her imagination to color the flowers.

Susan spent four years working on this rug. "Now and then I would grow frustrated with an element that wasn't working and several months would go by before I would pick it back up to work out the problem," she said. The most challenging part of this rug was hooking the faces. At times, turning the visual and the rug upside down helped Susan to overcome the difficulties. "I cried many tears as I struggled to hook my Mom's face to my satisfaction," she said.

In the Judges' Words

- *A near perfect adaptation of an old photo, including the woman who shut her eyes when the camera clicked*
- *Beautifully done*
- *Great use of color*

S usan DiPuma turned an old 2.5" x 3.5" photograph into this 41" x 32" wall hanging. The photograph was taken in 1941 on Easter Sunday. Pictured from left to right are Susan's Aunt Sally, Aunt Elizabeth, mother, and Aunt Janet. "They are dressed in their finest coats with corsages and incredible hats," she said. "I always loved this photo of three elegant women and decided to hook it as a tribute to my mom who has passed away."

Susan color planned the rug with guidance from Eric Sandberg and Pris Buttler. The photo was in black and white, so color planning was a little difficult. Susan ended

SUSAN DIPUMA
DULUTH, GEORGIA

Susan attended a gathering of rug hookers at a friend's house and left with a piece of backing, wool, a hook, instructions, and lots of encouragement. That was in 2006. Since then, Susan has hooked 44 items from mug rugs to floor rugs. Easter Sunday marks her first appearance in Celebration and her first award for her work.

Easter Sunday, 41" x 32", #3-, 4-, 5-, and 6-cut wool on monk's cloth.
Adapted from a family photograph and hooked by Susan DiPuma, Duluth, Georgia, 2012.

Eastman Still Life

With running a rose nursery, building a rug hooking business, and chauffeuring two children busy with ballet, baseball, and trumpet, it's no wonder Brigitta Phy chose to hook this "still" life. She adapted her pattern from prints of a painting done by her husband's grandmother, Blanca Eastman, in the 1950s. "I love the books on the table and the Mexican vase and the bright colors," she said.

Brigitta color planned the rug to match the original painting and chose colors from her stash of noodles. Most of the noodles had been dyed by her for use in previous projects utilizing a variety of techniques. She also had many different cuts to work with and many types of wool fabric. "The most challenging part was choosing the right hue of color from the endless bags of noodles to match the colors on my visual aid," she said.

Brigitta used directional hooking in the background wall, the vase, the books, and the table to give depth to the painting. "My favorite part of the rug is the bright red gladiolas," she said. "I love the contrast against the dark brown wall."

In hooking this rug, Brigitta learned a great deal about color, hue, and contrast and about shadows and light. "I also learned how to use a bag of scraps to find something that will work," she said, "even if it is not the exact color I thought I needed."

Brigitta credits her teachers, Capri Boyle Jones and Yanya Graham, for their direction and encouragement as she worked on this rug. To finish the piece, she whipped the rug with a dark green yarn to match the dark green hooked border. She rolled the backing forward and whipped it, eliminating the need to use rug tape on the back.

BRIGITTA PHY
SEBASTOPOL, CALIFORNIA

Brigitta is Jane Olson's granddaughter and grew up rug hooking. She recently started a rug hooking business and will be receiving her McGown Teachers Accreditation in June 2013. She has hooked about 40 rugs in the past 15 years. This is her first rug to be featured in Celebration.

Eastman Still Life, 23″ x 26″, *wool strips of varying size on monk's cloth. Adapted with permission from a painting by Blanca Eastman and hooked by Brigitta Phy, Sebastopol, California, 2012.* PHOTO BY BRUCE SHIPPEE

In the Judges' Words

- *The reflection of the light is captured perfectly with the changing colors on the wall.*
- *Clear understanding of use of value*
- *Nice variety of color*

Jim

appears monochromatic at first glance, a closer look at the loops shows that Timmie used a number of other colors to create a rich monochromatic effect, including purple, navy, brown, green, and even "some real black."

Timmie credits Betty with helping her to choose the best colors for the rug. "She was (as always) exactly right with her help for the background and mixing the colors for the 'blacks,'" she said. The background color was created by Betty; the "blacks" came from Timmie's stash. All of the colors came from a mix of mostly new and some recycled wool.

Timmie is especially pleased with how the figure of Jim came together. "It looks so much like him that no one need guess who it is," she said. Of course, the figure was also the biggest challenge, with the profile, head, and hat being particularly difficult. Timmie focused on completing as much of the figure as possible while she was at rug camp so she could tap the expertise of her teacher.

A background of directional hooking that incorporates very pale shades of the "blacks" used in the rug gives the background interest and helps it recede. The directional hooking allows the figure to be a prominent element in the rug's composition.

Timmie finished the rug with a herringbone stitch.

In the Judges' Words

- *Wonderful use of values to create a monochromatic evening*
- *Great story rug*
- *Invites you to ask who, when, where?*
- *Excellent light play*

The photograph on which Timmie Wiant based this rug hooking had been her favorite for years. It was taken by her son, Peter, as her husband Jim contemplated the Columbia River in Oregon. The contrast in the black and white photo and the contemplative stance of her husband intrigued her so much that she decided to hook the image into a rug.

Over the years, Timmie has become a regular at the Ocean City Rug School. She started the rug there under the guidance of Betty McClentic. While the finished rug

TIMMIE WIANT
ST. LOUIS, MISSOURI

Timmie decided to learn how to hook rugs after she bought two of Pearl McGown's rugs at auction and needed a third rug to balance out the room where she would display the other two. In the past 24 years, she has hooked about 80 rugs. Jim is her third rug to be featured in Celebration.

Jim, 16" x 23¹/₂", #3-, 4-, and 5-cut wool on linen. Adapted from a photo by Peter Wiant
of his father and hooked by Timmie Wiant, St. Louis, Missouri, 2012.

Lives Woven Together

Dianne Gill has always been attracted to antique textiles, their history, and the processes by which they were made. She thinks it is important to keep these traditions alive and to pass them on so they aren't lost or forgotten.

This deep love of all fiber arts led Dianne to combine rug hooking and weaving to come up with this rug based on antique Jacquard coverlet signature blocks in use between 1833 and 1863. She adapted four blocks to hook a memory rug illustrating her 38-year marriage to her husband, Earl.

A close look at the top of the rug will reveal Dianne's and Earl's names hooked into the background. In the lower right block (based on a design by Samuel Stiger), the star in the center represents Dianne and Earl, and the four medium stars closest to the large star represent their children. The lion (by Harry Tyler) depicts the Lion of Judah to symbolize Dianne's religious convictions. The eagle and stars block in the upper left (Matthew Rattray) represents their years as a United States military family. The final block shows the Craig Family Courthouse in Wyoming where Dianne and Earl moved so Earl could join the Wyoming Highway Patrol. Around each block, Dianne hooked a band of color that appears to be woven at each intersection.

Dianne color planned the rug, staying true to the indigo,

madder, fustic, and natural colors found in antique coverlets. She overdyed Dorr oatmeal and natural wool using the open pan mottle dyeing method for all the wool except the blue, which she purchased at a rug camp. Dianne incorporated beading on the courthouse roof and in the lion's mane.

"If I had to pick out my favorite part it would be designing the rug itself," she said, "looking through weaving and coverlet books, hunting for blocks, making the final selections, and then deciding how to adapt them. It was thrilling to see the rug come together."

DIANNE GILL
NEWNAN, GEORGIA

Dianne had admired hooked rugs in antique shops and knew she wanted to learn how to make them. A weaver, tatter, and lace maker, Diane sees rug hooking as a natural addition to her fiber journey. She has hooked 21 rugs since 2006. Lives Woven Together *is her first rug to appear in* Celebration.

Lives Woven Together, 30" x 33", #4- to 8-cut wool on linen. Designed and hooked by
Diane Gill, Newnan, Georgia, 2012. PHOTO BY JULIE TURNER BALDWIN

In the Judges' Words

- *Neatly hooked rows make this piece feel like the weaving it is meant to imitate*
- *Fun graphic design*
- *Good use of beading and line shading*
- *Love the roof!*

Mojo

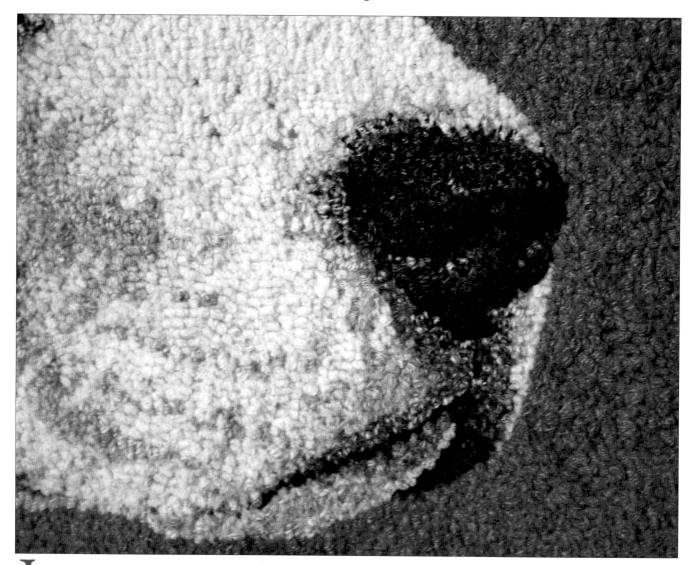

J udy Carter enjoys the challenge of capturing what she sees in photographs and reproducing it in hooked rugs. "I enjoy all styles and techniques of rug hooking," she said, "but my favorite subject is animals and my favorite style is realistic."

Judy planned the colors to match the colors in the original photograph of Mojo and chose all new wool for her

piece. Most of the wool is textured, as-is fabric. She penny dyed and dip dyed the remaining wool.

Her favorite parts of the rug are the muzzle and the brindle coloring. "I love the various colors in the dog and it was so much fun to mix the wools in order to match the coloring I saw in the photo," she said. She added a touch of pink and textured wool to recreate the look of the short hair at the muzzle.

Judy found the shadows and folds in the white neck to be the most difficult areas to hook. "I needed to use enough contrast to show the shadows while still hooking an almost all-white neck," she said.

Another difficult aspect of hooking this rug stemmed from the subject itself. "It's harder to hook a pet than a wild

In the Judges' Words

- *Incredible detail and the finest hooking*
- *Wonderful shading in fur*
- *Wonderful textures and colors*
- *Superb dog!*

Mojo, 25" x 21", #3- and 4-cut as-is and hand-dyed wool on rug warp. Adapted with permission from a photo by Leonard Feenan and hooked by Judy Carter, Willow Street, Pennsylvania, 2012.

animal," Judy said. "People are very attached to their pets, and you need to capture the look and personality of the animal." Hooking a technically correct, realistic dog or cat is not enough when the animal is a beloved companion.

Judy finished the rug by whipping the edges over cording. The completed rug is in the private collection of Leonard Feenan, but she often takes it to shows and classes as an example of shading and realistic portraiture.

JUDY CARTER
WILLOW STREET, PENNSYLVANIA

Judy celebrates 20 years of rug hooking this year. She learned to hook in a beginner's class by Pat Moyer. Since then she has hooked 107 rugs. Judy teaches regularly and runs Artisans Gallery. Mojo marks her 11th rug to be featured in Celebration.

Muck

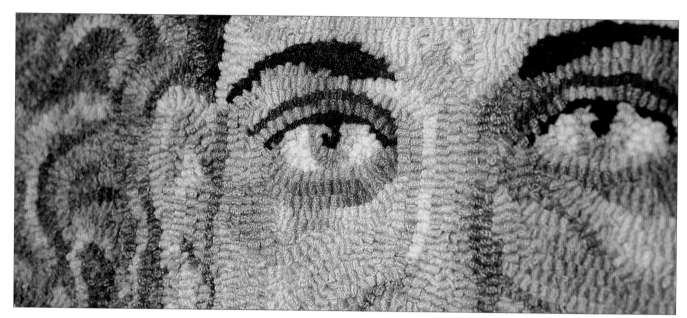

Denny Seyller started this rug in a three-day workshop on faces with Janet Williams. As he cast about for a face to hook during the class, he remembered a painting of his father from World War II. It had always hung in the hallway of his parents' home and had recently been moved to his brother's home. Denny knew immediately that this was the perfect subject for his rug.

Denny's brother took a digital picture of the painting for Denny to work with. From that photograph, Denny color planned the portrait to match the shades shown in the original painting. The guild members helped him decide on a background and a border color. He used new and as-is wool in #3 and #4 for the face and #4 and #5 for the uniform, background, and border. No wool was dyed specifically for this project.

As Denny worked to capture his father's expression and the highlights and shadows of the face, he found that he had to stretch his limited knowledge of rug hooking. Denny took his first class in 2007 and has hooked two rugs to date. "This turned into a much bigger project than I expected," he said. "It gave me a much higher appreciation of the works that have been created by other rug hookers."

For Denny, the most challenging part of hooking *Muck* turned out not to be his father's face but his uniform and his hair. Because those two elements are overwhelmingly brown, he had a difficult time finding the variety of wool colors he needed to create the three-dimensional look of the portrait.

To finish the rug, Denny whipped the edged with #6 strips of wool. The completed portrait hangs in his family's home. "I am happy with the eyes and nose, which I feel really capture my father's face," he said. "When I look at the rug, I see my father watching me."

In the Judges' Words

- *Excellent facial features*
- *Good handling of light and shadow*
- *Nice hair; cute curl*
- *Fabulous shading on the face*

DENNY SEYLLER
CHESAPEAKE, VIRGINIA

After 20 years of escorting his wife to guilds, rug shows, rug camps, teachers' workshops, and any other type of event within traveling distance that involved any type of rug hooking venture, Denny finally decided to try a class on his own. Muck is his second completed rug and his first rug to be featured in Celebration.

Muck, 21″ x 26³/4″, #3-, 4-, and 6-cut wool on linen. Adapted with permission and
hooked by Denny Seyller, Chesapeake, Virginia, 2012. PHOTO BY HOBBS STUDIO

Olifant

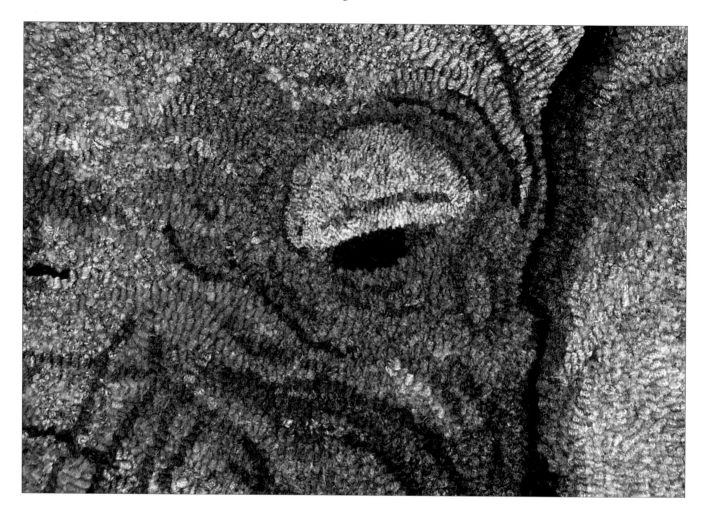

Val Flannigan's trip to South Africa is one she will never forget. This close-up portrait of an elephant sums up the emotion and excitement of her journey.

Val's son Colin took the picture upon which Val based the rug. His photo of an elephant they saw in their travels symbolized the enormity of the wilderness they visited and the amazing power and intelligence of this magnificent creature.

Val color planned the rug and dyed all of the wool using a variety of techniques, including a spot dye for the background and casserole and overdyeing as well as gradations and textures for the elephant. She used only new wool for this project and found that the most versatile piece was a gray and tan bouclé that allowed her to use both the right and the wrong sides. "It made for a great transition from one area to another," she said.

Val's favorite part of the rug is the eye. "I hooked it . . . and then after I had hooked all of his head, something didn't seem right," she said. "I redid the eye by sculpting it. I like the way it now adds to his overall expression."

Her biggest challenge was making the elephant look hot and dusty, an impression that was clearly conveyed by the photograph. "I dyed a great variety of wools, starting with camel-coloured wool, and added different amounts of gray," she said. "Then I started with gray and added different amounts of camel shades over that." She worked in only one area at a time and then moved to the adjoining area. She started with light values, then worked in the dark values, and finally added the medium values. She chose the spot-dyed wool for the background specifically because its "temperature" added to the dusty, hot feeling of the animal.

Val finished the rug with a whipped edge in a spot-dyed yarn.

Olifant, 20" x 18", #4-cut custom-dyed wool on linen. Adapted from a photograph by the artist's son and hooked by Val Flannigan, Kelowna, British Columbia, 2012.

In the Judges' Words

- *Great use of texture and color to create the elephant skin*
- *Masterful use of color and value*
- *Magnificent elephant*

VAL FLANNIGAN
KELOWNA, BRITISH COLUMBIA

Val always admired hooked rugs in magazines. When she visited a friend who was excited about her new "rug hooking experience," Val jumped at the opportunity to learn the art. Since 2000 she has hooked more than 100 large and small rugs. She owns White Hart Lane Studio. This rug is her first to be featured in Celebration.

Peonies and Birds

Kyoko Okamura lives in Japan where she finds it difficult to locate information and classes on traditional rug hooking techniques. Her limited knowledge of English also presents a barrier that Kyoko finds even more difficult to overcome. Fortunately, Kyoko met Chizuko Hayami, a rug hooking teacher who can help her learn more about rug hooking.

Kyoko's goal when she started this rug was to create a wall hanging that matched her Japanese-style tatami-matted room. As she considered the room, she realized that the Obi sash from her favorite kimono would provide an ideal starting point. She adapted elements of the pattern, colors, and motifs from the sash, then adjusted the size to fit her foundation and the display area.

To make sure her design was as pleasing as possible, Kyoko employed Ikebana, a traditional style of Japanese flower arranging. Kyoko arranged the flowers on her rug as one would arrange flowers following Ikebana: flowers in the center of the rug; open areas on all sides.

Kyoko kept the background plain and as even-toned as possible to make sure that the flowers received all the viewers' attention. Subtle curved lines at the bases of the flower stems suggest that the flowers are planted on a hillside. She used a #2-cut wool strip to trim and clarify the edges of the chrysanthemum petals.

Kyoko enjoys fine shading and used a number of swatch dyes and dip dyes for the petals and leaves. The background wool was casserole dyed. The border is vermillion silk from Kyoko's mother's kimono that she overdyed with brown. The finished piece hangs in the guest room at Kyoko's house.

In the Judges' Words

- Very traditional feeling
- Good shading in flowers
- Masterful handling of outline
- Nicely balanced and beautifully finished

KYOKO OKAMURA
TOKYO, JAPAN

Kyoko has hooked 34 rugs in the past 11 years. She is a member of the Chizuko Rug Hooking Studio, which holds an exhibition every 18 months. Peonies and Birds is her first rug to appear in Celebration; it is also her first rug to win an award.

Peonies and Birds, 40″ x 78″, #2- and 3-cut wool on linen. Adapted with permission from kimono fabric by Yoshio Nagira Company and hooked by Kyoko Okamura, Nerima-ku, Tokyo, Japan, 2011. PHOTO BY MASAYA OKAMURA

Rooster Fraktur

Cathy Williams decided on a fraktur as the topic for this rug simply because she wanted to learn more about the art form. A fraktur is described as a stylized, highly decorative watercolor or watercolor-and-ink painting in the Pennsylvania-German tradition, often bearing elaborate calligraphy and standardized motifs such as birds and tulips, to record family events such as baptisms and marriages. As she hooked, Cathy decided that her rug would commemorate her and her husband Waldo's sixtieth wedding anniversary.

Cathy turned to two books for reference: *Fraktur: Folk Art and Family* by Connie Earnest and Russell Earnest and *Fraktur: Tips, Tools, and Techniques for Learning the Craft* by Ruthanne Hartung. She chose one of the plate designs of a fraktur by an unknown artist as the basis of her pattern. She added letters and numbers to the design using a traditional fraktur alphabet.

Betty McClentic, Cathy's workshop teacher for this project, color planned and dyed the wool for this rug using samples that Cathy sent her. The blues, yellows, and red for the motifs and the border were dyed over new wool without any special techniques. The background color was created from a casserole dye. "I hooked the background straight across using the strips in the order of cutting," she said. "I wanted the background to look like it was vellum and quite spotty."

The background proved to be the most difficult part of this rug to hook. Cathy changed the background color after the initial color planning because she felt it needed to be several shades darker than she had originally planned to capture the look of old vellum. "Then I ran into the problem of losing the light yellow and orange as they were used," she said. "I had to move colors around, do some outlining, and use double lines of some colors so they would not fade into the background."

The result is a fraktur rug to be proud of—a lovely representation of a traditional art form.

CATHY WILLIAMS
LOS GETOS, CALIFORNIA

Whenever Cathy and her husband vacationed in Boothbay, Maine, she would choose a knitting project to work on while she was there. When they became seasonal residents, she switched to rug hooking. Rooster Fraktur won a blue ribbon at the Cumberland Fair and is her second rug to be featured in Celebration.

In the Judges' Words

- *Masterful #3 cut*
- *Beautiful fraktur colors*
- *Love the subtle differences hooked into a balanced design*

Rooster Fraktur, 31" x 26¹/₂", #3-cut wool on rug warp. Adapted with permission from an 1847 fraktur by an unknown artist in Fraktur: Folk Art & Family *by Connie Earnest and Russell Earnest and hooked by Cathy Williams, Los Getos, California, 2012.* PHOTO BY EVAN TCHELEPI

Symphony

Lynne Powell loves details, and most of her rugs have been pictorials and portraits done in #3, 4, and 5 cuts. After three busy, detail-filled years of beautiful scenes and smiling faces, Lynne decided she needed a break and turned to geometrics. However, she didn't leave any of the details behind.

Lynne started *Symphony* during a planned vacation at the Cambria Pines Rug Camp. "I wanted something fun and relaxing to work on," she said. "This pattern looked like a great opportunity to play with color. I loved the way the motifs fan out from the center."

As is usual for Lynne, her color planning evolved as she hooked the piece. "I pick a particular piece of wool or group of wools that I like and then sort out what works to create the best contrast," she said. "I add other pieces of color and texture as needed to make sure the motifs play together in a way that pleases me."

Lynne took some of her favorite wools from her stash to Cambria and then purchased more wool from the various

teachers and vendors at the camp. She chose four 6-value swatches to establish some continuity throughout the rug plus some spot dyes and dip dyes for accents and interest. Lynne considered using other materials, like ribbon and velvet, but found that the pattern had enough personality on its own.

A lot of that personality comes from the curved edges of the design. Binding those edges became the most challenging part of completing this rug. On advice from rug hooking friend Suzi Jones, Lynne ran a bead of Elmer's glue along the backing just beyond the last row of hooking, then trimmed and clipped the backing to ease the turns. The dried glue prevented the linen from unraveling. Instead of bending binding tape around the curves, Lynne cut a piece of white wool in the exact shape of the finished rug, cut out the middle, and sewed the remaining 2" strip to the underside of the rug to cover the folded edge of the backing.

The completed rug acts as a centerpiece for a round table in her dining room.

Symphony, 17¹/₂″ x 18″, #3-cut wool on linen. Based on Paisley and Flowers Doodle © blue 67design 2012. Used under license from Shutterstock.com. Hooked by Lynne Powell, Portland, Oregon, 2012. PHOTO BY ROBIN REID

In the Judges' Words

- *Good interpretation*
- *Fun with color*
- *Nice twinkle beading*
- *Love the creativity in this piece*

LYNNE POWELL
PORTLAND, OREGON

Portland Rug Hooking Guild members set Lynne up with a bag of wool, loaned her a frame, sold her a hook, and taught her how to "pull loops like ribbon candy" after a Gathering of the Guilds 20 years ago. This rug is her second to be featured in Celebration.

Woman in Sepia

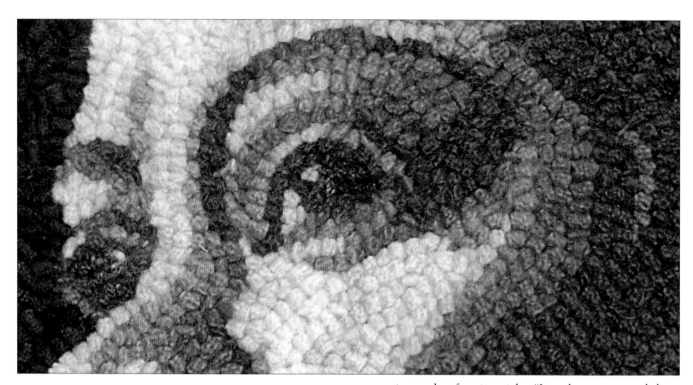

L yle Drier keeps a large folder of photos, drawings, and patterns that inspire or intrigue her. More than 20 years ago, she placed a photo of a woman that touched her heart into that folder. When she was accepted into Donna Hrkman's class at Sauder Village, Lyle decided to dig out that picture. "I thought it was the perfect time to bring her to life," she said.

Lyle had never done a portrait in sepia before and decided to color plan the rug in that color scheme. Donna dyed a 6-value swatch for the project. The dyeing was over new wool. Touches of a darker color grace areas of deep shadow while white highlights, like the woman's earring, catch the brightest light.

As one would imagine, the face was the most difficult part of this rug to hook. Lyle found it challenging to get the expression on her face just right. "It took some very subtle 'tweaking' to get it," she said. "Just changing a loop or two made all the difference."

In the end though, the expression became Lyle's favorite part of the rug. "I can't really describe it, but it touches my heart," she said. "She seems pensive and wise." The beaded border between the interior of the rug and the border pulls medium and light tones from the sepia portrait.

Lyle finished the rug with rug binding. Through hooking this piece she learned that 8 to 12 values of a color are not needed to achieve a shaded portrait—6 values worked just fine.

In the Judges' Words

- *Super concept*
- *Striking light, soft shadows*
- *Beading nice rug touch*
- *Effective directional hooking*

LYLE DRIER
WAUKESHA, WISCONSIN

After seeing hooked rugs featured on the pages of Woman's Day *magazine, Lyle decided that a hooked rug of her own making would be the perfect accent to the antiques in her home. Since that first rug in 1972, Lyle has completed 150 rugs.* Woman in Sepia *is her ninth rug to be featured in* Celebration.

Woman in Sepia, 15¹/₂″ x 17³/₄″, #3-, 4-, and 5-cut wool on linen. *Adapted from a portrait by an unknown artist and hooked by Lyle Drier, Waukesha, Wisconsin, 2012.*

Working on the Railroad

The photo that Trish Johnson used as the inspiration for this rug was taken in 1938 by her father, Fred Johnson, when he worked on the gang repairing and maintaining the track for the Canadian National Railways. At that time her father would have been 18 years old.

The original photograph sparked Trish's imagination because all of the men were identified and the photo was dated. The section of track from Capreol to Montreal holds many fond memories for her from her own childhood. Its disassembly in recent years made the creation of this rug even more important to Trish.

To make an attractive rug hooking pattern from the photograph, Trish significantly altered the original photo. She included only four of the six men in her father's picture,

she straightened out the track, and she replaced the bushes in the background with a map of the area. She had to angle the map so the rivers and place names wouldn't interfere with the men.

Trish color planned the rug from the black and white photograph. She only dyed one piece of fabric: the palest of greens for the background. All of the other wool was in her stash, including partial swatches of flesh tones left over from a previous project. She used plaids and textures from secondhand scarves for the workers' overalls, the track, and the gravel.

Design wise, she likes that each worker is a little different from the other in his dress and his expression. "Hooking wise, I like the red stripe on the socks and the

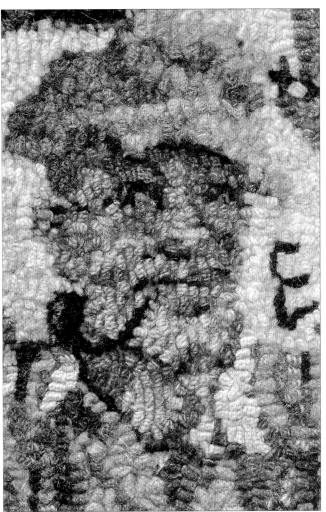

Working on the Railroad, 36½" x 16¾", #3-, 4-, and 5-cut wool on linen. Adapted from a photo taken by the artist's father, a photo of a track taken by the artist, and a map. Hooked by Trish Johnson, Toronto, Ontario, 2012.

red handkerchief, and the red strip on the bowl."

Trish said she learned several important things while hooking this rug. First, it would have been easier to start with new complete swatches of flesh tones than to try to use up partial swatches; second, that it's okay if detail gets lost in the shadows. And she learned it takes a long time to hook a rug like this: nearly 18 months.

In the Judges' Words

- *A lovely adaptation of an old photo*
- *Very effective background*
- *Great story rug*

TRISH JOHNSON
TORONTO, ONTARIO

Trish Johnson learned to hook rugs at her aunt's side when her aunt would allow her to "help" by hooking the sky. Since 1990, she has hooked 41 rugs. Trish is a teacher with the Ontario Hooking Craft Guild. Working on the Railroad is her seventh rug to be featured in Celebration.

Yellowstone

Roland Nunn chose this landscape because he liked the many levels of this scene. The dark colors of the buffalo grazing in the foreground keep the viewer's eyes engaged before he or she looks farther into the scene—to the foothills and the mountains in the distance.

To make the scene work, Roland concentrated on developing depth throughout the composition. He varied his direction of hooking from the foreground to the middle ground to the background to help give the perspective he needed to make the scene work. Vertical hooking in the foreground mimics the standing grasses of the plains. In the middle ground, Roland's hooking follows the undulating rise and fall of the mountains. The sky is hooked in horizontal rows.

Roland finds that choosing the right swatches is the most important part of hooking a landscape. He used 23 different swatches in this piece. "The use of a parent (base) swatch plus its transitional companions allows subtle variations in color with smooth transitions," he said. His use of closely colored swatches is especially apparent in the shading of the grasses.

To create the smooth look of the sky, Roland brush dyed a single piece of wool, cut it into strips, then hooked each strip in order as he built the sky. The shading from light to dark that moves from left to right across the sky is due to the shading on the single piece of fabric before it was hooked. Keeping the strips in the exact order of the original piece of wool is a challenge, but the result was well worth the effort as the sky came together in softly changing tones.

Yellowstone, 32" x 32", #3-cut wool on monk's cloth. Adapted with permission from a photograph and hooked by Roland Nunn, Orinda, California, 2012. PHOTO BY SCOTT MCCUE

In the Judges' Words

- *The beauty of the hills and grazing buffalo is beautifully captured in wool*
- *Effective use of color*
- *We are really at Yellowstone*

ROLAND NUNN
ORINDA, CALIFORNIA

Roland started hooking rugs at age 60 and now, 23 years later, he has completed 63 pieces in every style, from geometrics to florals to Orientals. He has been a regular attendee at the Asilomar Rug Camp for 15 years. Yellowstone is his seventh rug to be featured in Celebration.

Bigelow Pinecones

Autumn and all the things that go with it—acorns, leaves, pumpkins, and pinecones—are some of Susan Nash's favorite things. Susan had been toying with the idea of hooking a hit-and-miss rug. This pattern combines the two.

Susan began this rug in a three-day workshop sponsored by the Buckeye Rug Hooking Guild. She did all the color planning and dyeing, but received some much needed guidance from June Mikoryak when it came to hooking the pinecone motifs.

For the pinecones, Susan dyed 4-value swatches over plain and textured wool. Some of the hit-and-miss wools were left over from previous projects, but most of those wools are plain and textured, overdyed with the open pan method.

When she started hooking, Susan was intimidated by the pinecones and their realistic shading and small details. "But it turned out that the hit-and-miss squares were more difficult," she said. "I kept reminding myself of June's advice: 'dark against light, dull against bright.' I quickly learned that hit-and-miss only looks easy." Completing each square gave her a sense of accomplishment.

"The rug turned out just like I envisioned," she said. "Sometimes I start a rug with a mental picture of how I want it to look and it changes along the way. I am glad I was able to hook *Bigelow Pines* and stick to my original vision."

Because Susan likes to choose and hook patterns according to what she likes, she did not color plan this rug for a specific room in her house. "It seems to go nicely on the floor in my bedroom, and that is probably where it will stay," she said.

In the Judges' Words

- *Great pinecones*
- *Good combination of fine and wide cuts*
- *Fabulous finishing*
- *Beautiful color*

SUSAN NASH
NEW LEXINGTON, OHIO

This former and still occasional spinner and weaver learned to hook rugs during a break from practicing for a sheep-to-shawl contest. Co-owner of Somerset Wool, Susan has completed 30 rugs, and this rug's appearance in Celebration marks her first rug hooking award.

Bigelow Pinecones, 36" x 60", #3- to 8-cut wool on linen. Pattern by Keepsake Rug Patterns; hooked by Susan Nash, New Lexington, Ohio, 2012. PHOTO BY NASH IMAGING

Blackbird

Fritz Mitnick is a self-declared crow fancier, so she thinks of the birds in Kate Porter's pattern *Blackbird* as crows instead. But either way—crows or blackbirds—Fritz enjoyed hooking this rug. She finds hooking geometrics and working through the color plans that are associated with this type of rug both relaxing and inspiring.

The color planning for her version of the rug happened over the course of a year. "I threw wool on a pile for this rug for about a year," she said, "and I finally did the plan the day before leaving for the Ohio Rug Camp."

The wool she tossed on the pile was all as-is, both new and recycled, either purchased or from her stash. Although she enjoys dyeing, she did not dye any wool specifically for this rug. She used an antique paisley shawl and a handful of beads to add interest.

Working the paisley fabric into the design was a puzzle. "I never want to cut my old paisley shawls, and when I do, it bothers me to not be able to see their patterns," she said. "So by making little pillows of paisley and stitching the pillow to the backing, I could still see some of the wonderful old patterns." She notes that the paisley was too fragile to sew it directly to the linen, so she backed it with muslin.

Fritz's biggest challenge in hooking this rug was the triangular border. "I dreaded the monotony of hooking all those triangles and was stumped by what two colors should be used," she said. Fritz showed the rug to her co-teacher Susanne McNally, and that's when she found an answer: "I could use all the colors! I hate repetition, and this solution thrilled me."

The finished rug will spend about three months on the hallway floor off the living room and then will be retired for the remainder of the year to guard it against damage from sunlight.

FRITZ MITNICK
PITTSBURGH, PENNSYLVANIA

Fritz was so thrilled with winning a raffle at the Pittsburgh Rug Hooking Guild's show in 1997 that she started attending their lunchtime meetings. Three years later she quit her job as a librarian to make more time for rug hooking. This rug is her third to be featured in Celebration.

In the Judges' Words

- *Lovely use of antique paisley in the flowers*
- *Excellent use of color*
- *Very clean technique*
- *Nice finishing*

Blackbird, 24^1/$_2$″ x 44^1/$_2$″, #8-cut woven wool strips, antique paisley, and beads on linen. Pattern by Kate Porter/Loop de Loo Designs; hooked by Fritz Mitnick, Pittsburgh, Pennsylvania, 2012. PHOTO BY ALAN J. KING

Blackbird

Judy Stevens saw a smaller version of *Blackbird* years ago at a hooking event where the rug's designer was a vendor. She liked the pattern immediately, but felt she was still too new to rug hooking to tackle a piece with so many elements. Not only did she feel ready to hook the rug this year, she asked the designer to add two more motif blocks to create a larger rug!

Judy chose the colors for the rug to match the cream and rust colors of her family room and to include her two favorite colors, brown and blue. With those guidelines, Bea Brock dyed the wool and color planned the rug. She used a variety of standard dyeing techniques to get the even looks of the various colors.

Judy's favorite parts of this rug are the clean lines of the pattern and the geometric effect of the motifs. She hooked the rug so that some of the blocks are right-side up from any direction of approach.

The most difficult aspect of this rug was the border. "Hooking the wave in the outer border was challenging," she said. "I had changed the width of the border and had to redraw the depth of the wave."

Judy finished the rug by hand sewing navy blue twill tape to the back. The most important lesson she learned—how to effectively use value and contrast—is evident in the finished rug. "I struggle with values and color planning and can see in this rug how they can work well," she said.

JUDY STEVENS
WARREN, OHIO

Judy's "wonderful journey filled with great friends and rug hooking opportunities" started when she saw a display of hooked rugs at a county fair. She took two lessons with Beth Croup in 2005 and has hooked 30 rugs plus many small pieces. This rug is her first to be featured in Celebration.

In the Judges' Words

- *Good primitive hooking*
- *Perfect, beautiful loops*
- *Outlining very effective*
- *Nice complementary color scheme*

Blackbird, 55" x 25¹/₂", #6- and 8-cut wool on linen. Pattern by Katherine Porter; hooked by Judy Stevens, Warren, Ohio, 2011. PHOTO BY RICK PORTER

Bradley Primitive

Wide cuts are Sheri Bennett's passion. And in this rug-within-a-rug design, Sheri had the opportunity to do double the amount of hooking with wide-cut strips.

Sheri picked the colors for this rug with input from her teachers Ramona Maddox and Eric Sandberg. The outer border of the rug features a variety of greens and green-blue strips to create the leaves. Veins in the leaves along the edges are hooked in grays and gray-blues; leaves in the corners have darker green veins. Sheri used several shades of gray to complete the background of the outer border, following the outline of the leaves and flowers to complete the fill.

The left to right and top to bottom symmetry of the outside border is not duplicated in the center section of the rug, which adds greatly to the rug's interest and emphasizes the rug-within-a-rug feel. Here a solid brown background allows the lighter colored elements to stand out from the background. The top half and the bottom half of this central section are mirror images.

Sheri enjoyed creating the variety of motifs in this rug. The larger flowers allowed her to fill big areas with color while the smaller flower petals in the center were hooked with only a single strip of wool. The leaves feature shading that isn't found in the larger flowers.

Sheri bound the rug with the same wool used to hook the border. The finished rug occupies a spot in her bedroom at the foot of her bed.

In the Judges' Words

- *Pleasing variation of colors and textures in the leaves*
- *Good technique*
- *Nice balance of color*

SHERI BENNETT
CHATTANOOGA, TENNESSEE

Sheri learned about rug hooking at an international quilt festival in 1994 and signed up for a rug hooking class the following year. She has completed about 30 rugs and owns From Crook to Hook Wool Studio. This rug is her fourth to be shown in Celebration.

Bradley Primitive, 66¹/₂″ x 51″, #9-cut wool and antique paisley. Pattern by Fraser Rugs; hooked by Sheri Bennett, Chattanooga, Tennessee, 2012. PHOTO BY LANGSTON PHOTOGRAPHY

Colchester Bed Rug

To dye the wool for her rug, Cyndy chose Carnelian (rust rose) and Frosted Carnelian (gold), two colors similar to those in Ms. Hall's rug. She created a wide variety of colors with harmony and balance by using those two colors over different wools. For example, she overdyed a plain brown texture with a gold formula for the flower vase. For the foliage, she overdyed a handful of green, brown, bronze, and melon worms from old projects in one pot. The background is a royal blue spot dyed with the two colors and black.

The color planning and dyeing turned out to be the most challenging aspects of creating this rug. But once she got dyeing, everything fell into place. Mock shading and four values of a color can be very effective in wide-cut crewel motifs. "The dye pot did most of the work," she said. "The hooking was easy."

To put more focus on the crewel motifs, Cyndy altered the pattern to eliminate the inner border and outer rope. "At first I thought the flower motifs in the center were most pleasing," she said. "Then I thought the leaf border with the hearts was best. I just can't make up my mind." She does know, however, that limiting the palette to two colors over a variety of wools and simplifying the pattern allowed her to get the crewel look she wanted.

In the Judges' Words

- *Exquisite technique*
- *Great use of textures, dips, and value shading*
- *Wide cut well handled*
- *Love the warm colors*

Cyndy Duade saw a small version of this pattern at a teachers' workshop five or six years ago and knew that someday she would hook it as a wide-cut crewel.

Cyndy color planned the rug based on the colors of an embroidered bed rug by Lucretia Hall (shown in *The Art of Crewel Embroidery* by Mildred Davis). Ms. Hall based the design and colors of her rug on the flowers she grew in her own garden. "My objective was to create a wide-cut crewel-style rug that would echo an early American bed rug," Cyndy said.

CYNDY DUADE
NEW LONDON, NEW HAMPSHIRE

Friendship was the key that opened the rug hooking door for Cyndy. One friend brought her to a group meeting and another helped her buy equipment. She has been hooking rugs for 20 years and has now completed too many to count. This rug marks her second appearance in Celebration.

Colchester Bed Rug, 42" x 54", #8- and 8¹/₂-cut hand-dyed wool on linen. *Pattern by Jane M. Flynn;*
hooked by Cyndy Duade, New London, New Hampshire, 2012. PHOTO BY ANNE-MARIE LITTENBERG

Crewel Firescreen

Mary's teacher at camp, Carol Kassera, planned and dyed the colors for this rug, employing traditional crewel embroidery shades. "I love the colors," Mary said. "They are so bright and cheerful. It was a happy rug to hook."

The first motif Mary started to work on was the large mauve flower. "I remember feeling so lost for about the first two days of camp because this was such a challenge for me," she said. "But it felt awesome once I figured out the concept of shading." In addition to being thrilled with her new-found ability to hook the flowers, Mary likes the shading on the trunk of the tree of life and the shading in the hills.

An unexpected challenge came with the butterfly in the lower right-hand corner. She hooked it several times and still wasn't happy with the results. A co-worker drew the outline on a piece of paper, and only then did she see it clearly.

Mary learned several important techniques with this rug, including the difference between mock shading and traditional shading and how to hook one value alongside another to blend the colors. "I have been able to directly apply all that I've learned hooking this rug into my next project—and there isn't a single flower on it!" she said.

In the Judges' Words

- *Excellent shading*
- *Nice variation in the browns and sprinkling of color in the leaves*
- *Great technique*
- *Well balanced*

Mary McGrath started off hooking primitive rugs in a wide cut because they matched her home's décor. Recently however, most of the rugs she has hooked have been fine-cut pictorials or crewels. This rug fits the bill on both counts: fine cut and practical.

In anticipation of attending the Rock River Rug Camp in 2011, Mary chose *Crewel Firescreen*. "I fell in love with this beautiful crewel design," she said. "I wasn't ready to take on a realistic flower, so the colorful options a crewel pattern offered, combined with the whimsical design, really called to me."

MARY McGRATH
EAGLE, WISCONSIN

Mary only took on rug hooking after having a serious internal debate with herself about whether she could take on yet another hobby. The case for rug hooking was made, and Mary has since hooked 10 very large rugs. This rug is her second rug in Celebration.

*Crewel Firescreen, 28" x 34", #3-cut wool on monk's cloth. Pattern by Jane McGown Flynn;
hooked by Mary McGrath, Eagle, Wisconsin, 2012.* PHOTO BY MICHELLE ADAMSKI - ARTS CAMERAS PLUS

David's Vine

Diana Wilcox describes her attraction to this pattern as "love at first sight. When I see a pattern I love, I just jump right in," she said. "I would pour my coffee in the morning and sit and hook. Time slips away when you love your piece."

That love would pay off as Diana got farther into her project. While the colorful flowers and scrolls hooked up quickly, the vast background with all its dark wool was a different story. "I would hook a colorful piece and then do some background," she said. She knew that saving most of the background until the end of the hooking process would make the challenge of finishing the rug almost impossible.

As it was, completing this rug took Diana 14 months. She ran out of background wool and had to put the piece aside as she searched for matching wool.

To get the bright colors she wanted, Diana picked out paint chips and delivered them to Diane Stoffel, who dip dyed, spot dyed, and overdyed new wool in colors to match. The colorful design is not symmetrical, but the motifs do repeat themselves throughout the rug. Diana enjoyed the layout of the rug and found that she liked breaking the expectation of hooking a rug with mirrored elements.

Diana's favorite part of the rug is the two birds. "I own a parrot who makes me smile every day," she said. "The birds remind me of him."

Diana whipped the edges of the rug in a light gray to match the last rows of hooking. The finished rug will grace the foyer of her new home along with a matching 5' octagonal rug.

- Great details
- Beautiful light dips
- Colors work well with gray
- Well balanced asymmetrical design

DIANA WILCOX
ANNA MARIA, FLORIDA

Diana remembers her grandmother hooking as Diana watched as a young girl. Now retired, Diana returned to rug hooking as an enjoyable pastime. Since 2002, she has hooked 20 pieces, including 16 floor rugs. Her placement in Celebration is her first rug hooking award.

David's Vine, 116" x 56", #3-, 4-, and 5-cut wool on linen.
Pattern by Searsport Rug Hooking; hooked by Diana Wilcox,
Anna Maria, Florida, 2012. PHOTO BY IMPACT XPOSURES

Queen Mary

For Diane Luszcz, just getting started on *Queen Mary* was a challenge in and of itself. "I loved this design from the time I glimpsed it on the cover of the first rug hooking book I acquired: *The Lore and Lure of Hooked Rugs* by Pearl McGown," she said. Her first teachers encouraged her to start with something a little simpler and much smaller, so she set it aside. When she did decide she was ready to hook it, she broke her wrist and couldn't pull a loop until a year later. "During that time I planned it in my mind," she said, "so when I did start, it flew off my hook."

Diane dyed all new Dorr natural wool for this rug—except for one leaf that she had wool for in her stash. She used Moshimer Jacobean formulas as well as Jewel Tones and Color Flows to create swatches for the shaded leaves and flowers, a dip dye for the vines, and spot dyes for the accents. She thought she had enough wool, but one of the leaves is not like the others (and she's not sharing which one!).

In the Judges' Words

- Wonderful color and execution
- Great use of mock shading with values
- Dips and spots add well to the mix
- Super technique and finishing

DIANE LUSZCZ
HUDSON, NEW HAMPSHIRE

Diane walked into the Dorr Mill Store to take a braided rug class and walked out with a handful of rug hooking supplies. She finished the braiding class and the braided rug but has been rug hooking in the six years since. This rug is her third to be featured in Celebration.

Queen Mary, 38" x 72", #4-cut hand-dyed wool on linen. Pattern by Pearl McGown; hooked by Diane G. Luszcz, Hudson, New Hampshire, 2012.

Rooster

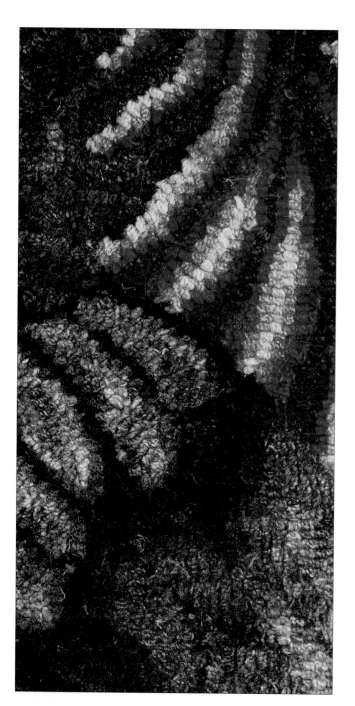

By her own admission, Laura McNeice "has a thing for roosters." The first rug she saw being hooked was a rooster rug. When it came time to design a rug of her own, there was no question: it had to be a rooster, and it had to be done in those same colors.

Laura asked her rug hooking teacher Loretta Scena to design the pattern for this rug. Loretta also color planned and dyed the wool. Loretta chose all new wool then spot dyed and dip dyed wool for the rooster and hand painted a piece of wool for the sky.

One of the most challenging aspects of the rug was hooking the rooster's feathers so they appear layered and shaded. Laura had to pay careful attention to reference materials and she constantly reviewed her loops to make sure her hooking was giving her the effect she wanted.

Laura enjoyed shading the purple coneflowers and the pansy at the bottom of the rug. "It was such a nice feeling when I stood back and they looked dimensional," she said. However, hooking them also proved a bit difficult. "The space for each petal was so small compared to the feathers that I had to really learn to use the play of lights and darks to keep them from growing beyond their borders." She was amazed and pleased by the sky. "The color just revealed itself as it went along—just like a sunrise."

Laura framed the rug as a wall hanging to protect it from her dog and foot traffic. She simply zigzag stitched the edges before having the piece mounted. The finished piece hangs on a wall between her kitchen and living room.

In the Judges' Words

- *Iridescent colors*
- *Beautiful painted sky*
- *Vibrant*
- *Love the colors*

LAURA MCNEICE
MASSAPEQUA PARK, NEW YORK

Laura is a hand piecing, appliqué, and quilting teacher and judge. She takes classes in rug hooking regularly from Loretta Scena and has attended classes by Michele Micarelli. Laura started hooking rugs in 2009. Rooster is her second rug hooked and her first rug to be featured in Celebration.

Rooster, 26³/4″ x 33″, #3-cut wool on linen. Designed by Loretta Scena and hooked by
Laura McNeice, Massapequa Park, New York, 2011.

Rowe Antique

Robin Winton Price purchased this pattern 20 years ago when she returned to hooking after her children graduated from high school. Robin's first lesson, when she was a teenager, was from her grandmother, a Southern belle who taught all her granddaughters what she called "the domestic arts."

Many of the patterns Robin chooses are antique-style rugs that feature scrolls. Gene Shepherd dyed the wool based on colors in his *Thistle* rug. "I had hooked a Celtic knot in a dip-dyed kind of style," she said. "It was blended end to end, and I wanted to try that technique on a scroll."

Robin started the rug at Cambria Pines Rug Camp. A broken ankle shortly after her return from camp gave her extra time to hook.

To separate the scrolls from the background, Robin outlined them with a strip of plaid wool. The central background color follows the shape of the border designated by the interior edges of the scrolls. Robin followed that pattern all the way to the center of the rug, giving even more of a sense of symmetry to the finished rug.

Overall, Robin was pleased with how this rug turned out. She likes how the colors flow from one part of the scroll to another and then back again and how the dark background colors make the colors in the scroll even brighter. Her commitments at work had given her little time to plan for camp. "I just picked this pattern without much thought," she said. "Everything clicked when I got there and saw the colors Gene had dyed."

Robin finished the rug with whipped edges and displays it on her living room wall.

In the Judges' Words

- *Good execution*
- *Striking color*
- *Masterful and rich background*
- *Lively coloring creates interest*

ROBIN WINTON PRICE
ANGELS CAMP, CALIFORNIA

Robin's southern grandmother taught her to hook rugs long ago, and over the past 20 years she's hooked too many rugs to count. This rug marks her first appearance in Celebration.

Rowe Antique, 31" x 58", #6-cut outline, #8-cut background, and #8.5-cut leaves on burlap.
Pattern by Charco; hooked by Robin Winton Price, Angels Camp, California, 2012.

Royalty

Rugs that resemble crewel work have a great appeal for Elaine Saxton, but they are also daunting. Elaine purchased the pattern for this rug and then let it sit for several years, looking at it now and then, working up the courage to start hooking.

Royalty marks her first attempt at a rug with a dark background. She chose Pearl McGown's eggplant formula over medium gray wool for the background. The leaves came from a dip dye in her stash, and the vines were hooked from a swatch. She enlisted the help of Suzanne Sandvik to dye the yellows, reds, and blues of the flowers.

Elaine is happy with the balance of color in the finished rug. "During the hooking process certain colors seemed to take over," she said, "but when I finished, I saw there was a good balance." She was pleased that she resisted the urge to reverse hook portions of the rug in response to that initial feeling of unbalance.

Elaine faced two challenges in completing this rug. First, she found it difficult to see the right and wrong side of the dark wool. She is not sure that she ever did make the right choice, but decided it wasn't an issue with this shade of wool. The other challenge was that the lightest shades of the swatches just faded away. "I couldn't use the first two or three strips in the swatch," she said. "I assumed the opposite: that the dark would get lost in the dark background. In this rug that wasn't true."

After 10 months and several starts and stops, Elaine completed the rug. It is displayed on the floor of her living room.

ELAINE SAXTON
HOWELL, MICHIGAN

Elaine and her husband found a display by the McGown Rug Hookrafters during Fall Festival in Clinton, Michigan. She was so fascinated that she signed up for lessons on the spot. Since 1993 she has hooked nearly 60 rugs. Her selection for Celebration *is her first rug hooking award.*

In the Judges' Words

- *Great hooking and pattern interpretation*
- *Beautiful shading and color plan*
- *Good control of values*
- *Well-balanced color*

Royalty, 34" x 54", #3- and 4-cut wool on burlap. Pattern by Mildred Sprout (Jane Olson);
hooked by Elaine Saxton, Howell, Michigan, 2012.

1845 Fraktur Eagle

Kristi Roberts enjoys the simplicity and "freeness" she feels when she is hooking primitive rugs—and this pattern featuring a fraktur eagle seemed to be just the project to take to a workshop in Missouri. "I was really looking for something patriotic," she said. "What I liked most about the pattern was the lack of detail, which would allow me to hook the rug in #8.5- to 9-cut strips."

Rhonda Manley of Black Sheep Wool Designs, the workshop's teacher, helped her to color plan the rug based on an antique painting of an eagle. The entire painting was in red, white, and blue. While both women liked those colors, Rhonda suggested hooking the wings and tail in browns instead to allow only the shield to be hooked in red, white, and blue. The coloration in the finished piece puts the viewer's focus on the shield first and the eagle second.

Kristi chose mostly as-is wool for this rug, although she did use a small amount of dyed wool. Her biggest challenge

in completing the piece was to ensure that the head, beak, and feet of the eagle show up against the light background. She outlined the eagle's head in the same color as the background but changed the direction of the loops to make it stand out. The beak and feet are a darker shade than she originally intended, to give them greater visibility.

"The greatest thing I learned in hooking this rug," she said, "is that there are many shades of 'light' and that I like 'dirty light,' and that these shades of wool used together make a perfect background."

Kristi doesn't have one favorite part of this rug. Instead, she admires the rug as a whole and is pleased with how all of the individual elements join together to make a cohesive image. She whipped the edges with yarn, and the finished piece is displayed on the floor of the family room where Maggie (her dog) seems to like the finished rug just as much as Kristi.

1845 Fraktur Eagle, 36" x 36", #8- and 9-cut wool. Adapted from an antique fraktur and hooked by Kristi Roberts, Houston, Texas, 2011.

In the Judges' Words

- *Great mix of beautiful textures in beautiful American color plan*
- *Good attention in the background strips to show the eagle's head and beak*
- *Coloring has an antique feel*

KRISTI ROBERTS
HOUSTON, TEXAS

Kristi and her sister were so enamored by the beautiful rugs in Soni Castle's studio that when Soni told them the beginners' classes were full, her sister offered to pay for private lessons for both of them. After that initial $25 in 1996, Kristi has hooked more than 80 items from rugs to chair mats. This rug is her first to be chosen as a finalist for Celebration.

Berks County

mottled effect. Some of her first efforts were too bright, so she overdyed them in taupe to tone them down. "Trial and error created the background," she said. She purchased the plaid wool that appears in small bits throughout the rug.

The background was difficult to hook. "Medium colored backgrounds can be tricky as it is hard to get the motifs to contrast without making them too garish and bright," she said. "Picking and choosing when to hook in some of the brighter strips created the look I wanted. I was happy with the balance I found."

The birds, however, were even more challenging. She tried several color variations, including gray (which had too much blue in it for her liking) and then gray and brown (which didn't stand out well against the background). "I finally decided on coral and purple birds, which stood out when I made them a bit brighter than the background," she said.

Jan especially likes the way the leaves turned out. She had never hooked with solids and textures before and was delighted with the effect of creating a light to dark palette from the combination. "Hooked textures can fool you by appearing darker than the solid fabrics," she said.

In the Judges' Words

- *Wonderful color choice*
- *Beautiful use of textures*
- *Lovely swirl in the background*
- *Perfection*

Jan Winter has been interested in Pennsylvania Dutch arts in general and frakturs in particular for a number of years. When she decided to design *Berks County*, Jan opted to break from tradition—but just a little. The elements are still true to the traditional fraktur designs; however, the colors are wildly different. "Frakturs traditionally used red, blue, yellow, and black on parchment paper," she said. "I chose a dusty pink background with some mottling for interest, and neutral colors for leaves."

Jan dyed all the solid colored wools in the rug. She added lots of small pieces of natural wool to one pot to create a

JAN WINTER
HOLLYWOOD, CALIFORNIA

After taking a quilting class where she learned to make a quilt that resembled a hooked rug, Jan walked away interested in not quilting but rug hooking. Since 1992 she has hooked 25 rugs, mostly in the primitive style. She received several blue ribbons at the Los Angeles County Fair. This is her eighth rug to appear in Celebration.

Berks County, 36″ x 22″, #6- and 8-cut wool on monk's cloth.
Designed and hooked by Jan Winter, Hollywood, California, 2012. PHOTO BY JOE WOLCOTT

Checkered Jardiniere

Cindy Trick is a florist by trade and has worked in the floral industry for the past five years. Not surprisingly, she finds that rug patterns including flower arrangements of some type are the most appealing. "Flower rugs are my favorite," she said. "I naturally gravitate toward those, especially the ones with baskets."

Cindy color planned the rug to incorporate the toned-down colors that are commonly seen in primitive rugs. She used new and recycled overdyed wool and wool paisley. The background is hooked with off-the-bolt wool.

Adding the reds and golds of the flowers provided dots of color against the darker brown background. Cindy used the paisley to outline the bowl, fill the center of the leaves, and accent several of the large flowers. The lighter colored wavy lines in the background highlight the flower arrangement and add interest to the background. Cindy was careful to follow the outline of the leaves, flowers, and vase as she worked her way out from the flower arrangement to the inside border of the rug.

The most difficult part of the rug to hook—the bowl—is also Cindy's favorite part of the finished piece. The bowl was drawn as a checked surface in the original pattern, but

she decided to hook it differently. She varied the tones on the surface of the bowl to give the impression of depth, with highlights and shadows. The paisley outline separates the bowl from the background and reflects the colors in the flowers. "The bowl was the last thing I hooked," she said. That gave me more time to decide how I wanted to hook it."

Cindy whipped the edges with yarn. The rug is currently displayed in her living room.

CINDY TRICK
BEAVERCREEK, OHIO

Since learning rug hooking under the direction of Dottie Beach in 1987, Cindy has hooked over 125 pieces, including rugs, wall hangings, table mats, bags, and 3-D art. She is a member of ATHA and the Miami Valley ATHA Guild. Her rug's appearance in Celebration marks her first rug hooking award.

Checkered Jardiniere, 35^1/$_2$" x 20^1/$_2$", #6-, 8-, and 8^1/$_2$-cut wool on linen. Pattern by Kris Miller (Spruce Ridge Studios); hooked by Cindy Trick, Beavercreek, Ohio, 2012. PHOTO BY BRIAN SWARTZ

Four Square Floral

Ironically, Betty Rafferty, who became a McGown certified rug hooking teacher this year, started out teaching school as a profession when she was a young mother. "I tried teaching for one year and found that not to be my calling, so I became a stay-at-home mom of three," she said. Now that she's discovered a passion for rug hooking, she finds that she has a desire to share it with others.

After five years of hooking rugs, Betty volunteered to make a hooked piece for her son and daughter-in-law's newly remodeled kitchen. Her daughter-in-law picked this pattern to match the color and feel of their new space. Rug hooker Mary Johnson used paint chips and pictures to spot dye all new wool in the shades Betty needed.

Betty took extra care with the tulips. "I loved doing the center ring of tulips," she said, "because they are my daughter-in-law's favorite flower. I tried to be creative in the hooking."

Betty had two challenges to overcome as she hooked this rug: the weight of the rug and the endless brown background. Knowing that the rug was going to a pair of special people for a special reason kept Betty hooking. "The longer I hooked, the more I liked the rug," she said. In the end, she was sad to part with her creation but knows that it will have a good home. "There will always be more rugs," she said.

Betty bound and whipped the edges with twill tape and yarn. The finished rug hangs on the wall in her son and daughter-in-law's newly expanded kitchen.

In the Judges' Words

- *Effective use of primitive color*
- *Clean and crisp*
- *Beautiful textures*
- *Nice use of colors and neutrals*

Four Square Floral, 40" x 40", #8-cut wool on monk's cloth.
Designed by Mary Johnson; hooked by Betty Rafferty, North Mankato, Minnesota, 2012. PHOTO BY ARTCRAFT

BETTY RAFFERTY
NORTH MANKATO, MINNESOTA

While strolling through the boutique shops in a river town, Betty happened upon a shop owned by a rug hooker. The woman's love of rug hooking and enthusiasm were contagious, and Betty left with a kit, which she worked on through a community education class. She has completed 30 rugs in the past 5 years. This is her first rug hooking award.

Give Ye Thanks

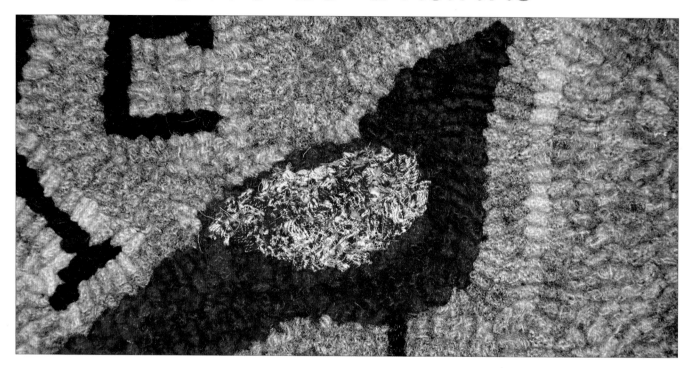

The tradition in Sandra Katulak's family is that she always hosts Thanksgiving dinner. "I saw this pattern at Sauder Village a few years ago," she said. "I fell in love with it and thought it would be perfect to have this special rug on display during our holiday dinner."

Sandra worked with Sally Kallin to color plan the rug during a workshop. After combining some of the wool Sandra brought from her stash and some suggestions from Sally, Sandra was ready to get started. She chose mostly new wool, textured as well as dyed, plus some paisley. "I love using antique paisley in my projects," she said. "It's fun to think that this fabric was potentially used or worn by a woman who lived a hundred or more years ago. Now the fabric has new life and can be enjoyed by the women of today."

For Sandra, finishing is always the hardest part of completing a hooked rug. "I love the look of whipped edges, but sometimes I have to fight with the rug to ensure the edging is uniform and that the rug lies flat," she said. For finishing this rug, Sandra used a large wooden needle that was slightly curved and helped to control the tension of the yarn as she whipped the edges. She steams her rugs as she is whipping to encourage the rug to lie flat.

Overall, Sandra is pleased with the finished rug. "I love the colors," she said. "They came together so beautifully and

the result is a rug that I can display proudly during Thanksgiving, my favorite family gathering. The rug represents my thankfulness for my family, friends, and life's blessings." The finished rug is displayed in her dining room and swapped out for other rugs during the rest of the year.

In the Judges' Words

- *Beautiful color plan*
- *Good use of textures*
- *Wonderful primitive scene*

SANDRA A. KATULAK
CENTERVILLE, OHIO

Sandra knew she was in trouble when she finished the rug hooking class she really hadn't want to go to and ended up in love with everything about the art. She started rug hooking in 2002 and has finished 15 rugs and one stool. Her rug's inclusion in this year's Celebration *is her first rug hooking award.*

Give Ye Thanks, 27¹/₂″ x 36″, #8-cut wool on linen.
Pattern by Kris Miller; hooked by Sandra A. Katulak, Centerville, Ohio, 2012.

Lucinda's Quilt

Jasmine Benjamin is working on an "old 100 year look," which means blending different textures and mixing them—the opposite of detailed shading—to fit the Old New England feel of her home's décor. "The first time I saw this design I saw possibilities and colors started swirling in my head," she said. "When it came time to hook a rug for the short front hallway of her 156-year-old New England Gingerbread Cottage, I immediately thought of this and decided it would make a good camp project."

Jasmine went to camp with enough wool to hook two runners and a very clear picture in her mind of how she wanted the finished piece to look. "I knew I wanted to use a lot of texture wools for the animals and a red brick house in the center, a dark mixed-tweed for the border, a split background, and blended blocks of different background colors to give it that 100-year-old look."

Most of the wools Jasmine hooked into this rug were over-dyed tweeds. A leg from an over-dyed Salvation Army uniform and over-dyed camels and tweeds from her mother provided her with the background (eight different oatmeals), some of the trees, the sky (three different over-dyed textures), and the border. An as-is tweed was perfect for the brick house. In addition, she bought one spot-dyed piece specifically for the windows.

Jasmine tried a new technique called "annagodlin'" for the windows. "Basically you hook three or four loops in one direction and then change direction for another three or four loops, leaving no ends visibly clipped," she said. "It's a time consuming and wool spending method but it's great for windows."

Her favorite part of *Lucinda's Quilt* is the split background, starting with the grass under the house and moving to the oatmeal colored middle ground and the sky at the top. "The swirling or 'S' background is not a traditional runner background," she said.

In the Judges' Words

- Good color choice
- Lovely mix of spots and textures
- Fabulous bricks
- A master's hand gives this rug a lot of character

JASMINE BENJAMIN
WEST BROOKFIELD, MASSACHUSETTS

Jasmine was practically born with a hook in her hand. She was born on a Wednesday, which was hooking class day, and her mother, Jeanne Benjamin, is a certified instructor. Jasmine learned to hook rugs at age 7. In the past 26 years she's hooked 60-some rugs. Lucinda's Quilt is her second rug to be featured in Celebration.

Lucinda's Quilt, 69" x 25", #6- and 8-cut hand-dyed wool on linen. Pattern by Barbara Carroll; hooked by Jasmine Benjamin, West Brookfield, Massachusetts, 2012. PHOTO BY JEREMIAH BENJAMIN

My Rug Hooking Story

Deborah Walsh packs a lot of wonderful memories into this Azeri-style rug started in a class with Norma Batastini. Azeri rugs were traditionally woven in a profusion of bright primary colors by the Azeri and Kurd tribespeople of Turkey. Deborah follows in that tradition as she surrounds the tale of her rug hooking life with an eye-catching border.

In the top portion of the central design, the pansy logo signifies her first class with Stephanie Krauss. The red barn is from Shelburne, Vermont, where she took a dye class that is represented by the hanging wool. In the middle of the rug are several places where Deborah has traveled to hook rugs with others: Oakside, a cultural building in Bloomfield, New Jersey; the ESC School in Lambert, New Jersey; and the Marriott where her family and friends hold their own rug hooking retreat every February. The bottom portion of the rug represents Chalfonte, where she has attended Rugs by the Sea summer camp for several years. Deborah includes multiple images of three people throughout the central portion of the rug: herself; her sister, Gail; her mother, Jeanne; and her friend, Amy. Deborah also includes miniature versions of some of her favorite hooked rugs.

The butterflies hooked in a short row in the middle of the rug to the right are remembrances of rug hookers who were important to Deborah who have passed away, including her stepmom's mother, Julia (pink butterfly), and her good friend Emily (blue and white butterfly).

Norma dyed the wool for the Azeri class, and Deborah chose the colors she wanted to use in her rug. Deborah is especially fond of the richness of the orange-red wool. However, picking the colors for the border was a challenge because she had so many to choose from. "I ended up photographing the rug in process to look at the border colors," she said. "That sometimes helped to see what worked and what didn't. And then I did some reverse hooking for the choices that didn't work well."

In the Judges' Words

- *A story that resonates with all of us!*
- *Good color choices and hooking*
- *Good balance of colors*
- *Fun story "Azeri" rug*

DEBORAH WALSH
CRANFORD, NEW JERSEY

Deborah's stepmom made kits for her twin stepdaughters who loved the experience so much that they went out to purchase materials for "big rugs" the very next day. In the 13 years since, Deborah has hooked 45 rugs. My Rug Hooking Story *is her second rug to appear in* Celebration.

Rug Hooking Story, 41" x 59", #3-, 4-, and 6-cut wool on linen.
Designed and hooked by Deborah Walsh, Cranford, New Jersey, 2012. PHOTO BY IMPACT XPOSURES

Oliver Cromwell

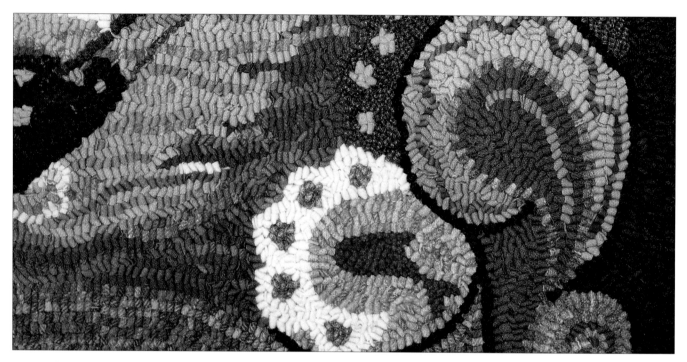

The *Oliver Cromwell* was launched on June 13, 1776, in Essex, Connecticut, as part of the naval force that defended the colonies during the American Revolution. All of the colonies' ships were captured or destroyed by 1779, including the *Oliver Cromwell*, which captured nine British ships before it was captured in turn by the British near Sandy Hook after a two-hour battle with three ships and a brig from the opposing forces. It is this magnificent ship that Julie Reilly wanted to hook as a gift for her sister, Linda.

"She asked me to hook a ship to be hung in her master bedroom at her lake house," Julie said. "I worked on the ship for a year and finished it for her as a surprise on her birthday. Even though she had helped plan the rug, she didn't know that I was finishing it for that occasion."

Julie used all new wool and sought the help of Katie Hartner to color plan the rug. She and her sister met with Katie to talk about the colors that would be part of the house, and the trio then pulled wools that would match or complement the color scheme.

The most challenging part of the rug for Julie to hook was the water. "I wanted movement and had to work with the colors to try and portray that," she said. This rug is also the largest one Julie has ever hooked, so she had to find a way to deal with the weight of the rug. Her solution was to get a new hooking frame, which made the process much easier.

Julie finished the rug with binding tape, and it is displayed over the bed in the master bedroom of her sister's house. "Linda designed her room around the rug, and it is beautiful where it is hung."

In the Judges' Words

- *Good use of texture*
- *Good color plan*
- *Love the gold fishes!*

JULIE REILLY
TYLER, TEXAS

Julie's favorite purse for years was hooked, but she had no idea what she was carrying until a friend pointed it out to her. After her friend invited her to a rug hooking group meeting and shared what goes into rug hooking, Julie was officially "hooked." She has hooked 20-plus rugs since 2008, and this is her first award.

Oliver Cromwell, 49" x 37", #8-cut wool on linen;
Pattern by Edyth O'Neill; hooked by Julie Reilly, Tyler, Texas, 2012. PHOTO BY BOB GEORGE

Rags to Riches

Ann Deane did not hook *Rags to Riches*. Instead, she won it. *Rags to Riches* was designed by Georgeanne Wertheim as the raffle rug for the 2012 Angela Pumphrey Workshop sponsored by the Heart of Texas ATHA Chapter in San Antonio, Texas. The theme of that year's workshop was Rags to Riches.

Georgeanne color planned the rug based on traditional colors for primitive hand-hooked rugs. The design is symmetrical and is based on several quilt block patterns, including Courthouse Steps. Georgeanne used new wool complemented by a small amount of hand-dyed purchased wool. The rug was hooked by members of the Heart of Texas Chapter of ATHA: Denice Brockmeyer, Liz Fox, Carol Gillingham, Lu Lacy, Tricia Travis, and Georgeanne Wertheim; each woman had one week to complete her assigned part of the rug. Ann Deane won the rug as part of the workshop's raffle.

Collectively, the group felt that the precision needed to hook the Courthouse Steps is the most impressive part of the rug. All of the rows had to be even in width, and the edges had to be ruler straight. The group worked hard to create clean perpendicular joints and evenly spaced parallel lines throughout the rug. "We learned the importance of balancing values of wool and the importance of hooking exact, straight lines to achieve a geometric look," the group said. The tulips in the center also had to appear symmetrical, but the curved edges allowed a leeway there that was not possible in the straight-line elements of the rug.

The rug is finished with rug tape to stabilize the diagonal sides. Ann, who calls herself the "lucky winner" to have received such a gorgeous work of art, displays the rug on her grandmother's round dining table.

In the Judges' Words

- *Very good color selection*
- *Big, beautiful textured loops*
- *Octagon shape complements the geometry of the design*
- *Impressive workmanship*

Rags to Riches, 36" octagon, #8-cut wool on linen. Designed by Georgeanne Wertheim and hooked by members of the Heart of Texas ATHA chapter; in the collection of Ann Deane, Murchison, Texas, 2012. PHOTO BY ED DEANE

HEART OF TEXAS
ATHA CHAPTER
Rags to Riches was a collaborative effort by this group of rug hookers. Created as a raffle rug, it was won by Ann Deane of Murchison, Texas, who entered it into Celebration.

ADAPTATION

Bunny Bling, 51" x 32¹/₂", #3- to 8-cut wool on linen.
*Adapted with permission from Alison Friend artwork and hooked
by Annette Cochrane, Omaha, Nebraska, 2012.*

PHOTO BY TERRY KOOPMAN

COMMERCIAL

Fall Challenge, 20" x 20", #3-, 4-, and 6-cut wool on linen.
*Designed by Faith Williston for House of Price; hooked by
Martha Lowry, Houston, Texas, 2012.* PHOTO BY JAMES LOWRY

ORIGINAL

Curb Stones and Crosses, 35" x 47", #6- and 8-cut new and
recycled wool and wool/silk roving on linen. Designed and
hooked by Holly Kingdon, High River, Alberta, Canada, 2012.

COMMERCIAL

*Africa's Gift, 43" x 28¹/₂", #4-, 5-, and 6-cut wool on monk's cloth. Designed by Jane McGown Flynn;
hooked by Elise Roberts, Orange, California, 2012.* PHOTO BY GENE SHEPHERD

PRIMITIVE

*A Sunny Garden, 39" x 24", #8-and 8¹/₂"-cut wool on linen. Designed by Searsport Rug Hooking;
hooked by Kathy Stephens, Houston, Texas, 2012.* PHOTO BY KRISTI ROBERTS AND DOUG ROBERTS

ORIGINAL

A Mother's Heartstrings, 37" x 30", #4-, 6-, and 8-cut wool
on linen. Designed and hooked by Brenda Stovall Cain,
Gainesville, Georgia, 2011. PHOTO BY COURTNEY CAIN RUE

ORIGINAL

Ginger, 29" x 21¾", #6- and 9.5-cut wool on linen.
Designed and hooked by Carolyn Ells, Montreal,
Quebec, Canada, 2011. PHOTO BY BRIAN A. MURPHY

PRIMITIVE

Four Guardians, 126" x 80",
wool and antique paisley on
cotton warp. Designed and
hooked by Carol W. Murphy,
Hopkinton, New Hampshire,
2011. PHOTO BY BECKY FIELD

ORIGINAL

Foxglove, 30¹/₂″ x 25¹/₂″, #3- and 4-cut. Designed and hooked by Sharon A. Kollman, Glen Arm, Maryland, 2012.

PRIMITIVE

Shaker Carrier with Flowers, 25″ x 16″, #8-, 8¹/₂″-, and 9-cut wool on linen backing. Designed by George Kahnle; hooked by Irene Shell, Woodinville, Washington, 2011. PHOTO BY J. DENNY

COMMERCIAL

Masterful Morris, 35″ x 54″, #3-cut Dorr wool on linen. Designed by Jane McGown Flynn; hooked by Chizuko Hayami, Setagaya, Tokyo, 2012.

PRIMITIVE

Native American Series #3 Southeast Woodlands, 24″ x 59″, #5- to 10-cut wool on linen. Designed and hooked by Joan D. Sample, Woodinville, Washington, 2012.

ORIGINAL

Life in the Garden, 39″ x 23″, multiple cuts of various alternative fabrics, wool, and beads. Designed and hooked by Margaret Miller, Richmond Hill, Ontario, Canada, 2011.

PHOTO BY MARY ANN DONAHUE

ORIGINAL

The Alice Rug, 60″ x 35″, #8-cut wool and hand-cut paisley on linen. Designed and hooked by Kathleen Harwood, Montrose, Pennsylvania, 2011.

PHOTO BY VAN ZANDBERGEN PHOTOGRAPHY

ORIGINAL

Above: *Painted Prairie*, 29¹/₂″ x 56″, wool fabric and wool yarn. Designed and hooked by Holly Lynn McMillan, Roca, Nebraska, 2011.

PHOTO BY BRAD CHRISTIANSEN

COMMERCIAL

Left: *Quaint*, 37″ x 26″, #3-cut wool on monk's cloth. Designed by House of Price; hooked by Karen Maddox, Kerrville, Texas, 2012.

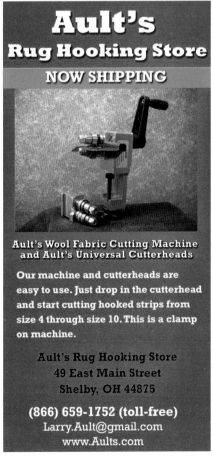

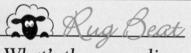

ADVERTISING INDEX